POWER ENGLISH

BASIC LANGUAGE SKILLS FOR ADULTS

3

Dorothy Rubin

TRENTON STATE COLLEGE

CAMBRIDGE Adult Education
Prentice Hall Regents, Englewood Cliffs, NJ 07632

PHOTO CREDITS
CHAPTER ONE: American Red Cross
CHAPTER TWO: Florida Department of Commerce
CHAPTER THREE: AP/Wide World Photos
CHAPTER FOUR: Swift & Company
CHAPTER FIVE: Irene Springer

Editorial supervision: Timothy Foote
Production supervision: Alan Gold
Manufacturing buyer: Mike Woerner

© 1989 by Prentice-Hall Regents
Published by Prentice-Hall, Inc.
A Division of Simon & Schuster
Englewood Cliffs, New Jersey 07632

Printed in the United States of America

10 9 8 7 6 5 4 3 2

ISBN 0-13-688466-0

Prentice-Hall International (UK) Limited, *London*
Prentice-Hall of Australia Pty. Limited, *Sydney*
Prentice-Hall Canada Inc., *Toronto*
Prentice-Hall Hispanoamericana, S.A., *Mexico*
Prentice-Hall of India Private Limited, *New Delhi*
Prentice-Hall of Japan, Inc., *Tokyo*
Simon & Schuster Asia Pte. Ltd., *Singapore*
Editora Prentice-Hall do Brasil, Ltda., *Rio de Janeiro*

CONTENTS

Power English: Basic Language Skills for Adults is a ten-book series dedicated to helping adults at the ABE level develop their skills in usage, sentence structure, mechanics, and composition. *Power English* consists of the locator test for the series, eight text/workbooks, and a series review book.

There are five chapters in each of the text/workbooks. The several lessons in each chapter cover a variety of writing skills. The comprehensive Chapter Reviews and Posttests in each book provide skill reinforcement. To facilitate diagnosis, there are Progress Charts for recording students' Chapter Review and Posttest performance. Answers are in a special section at the end of each book. The section can be left in the book so that students can check their own work, or since its pages are perforated, it can be removed.

Power English is comfortable for an adult whose reading level is between 4.0 and 8.0. Each lesson is a simple and concise presentation of a specific writing skill. In the instructional portion of a lesson, under the heading **Read the following** students study examples of a specific writing skill at work. Under **Did you notice?** they read short, clear explanations of the skill at hand. Because a typical lesson reinforces and expands upon skills taught in earlier lessons, a section called **Do you remember?** reviews pertinent rules and concepts previously presented. The

Try it out portion of a lesson provides exercise for applying and practicing the new and reviewed skills.

Power English encourages the rapid and enjoyable acquisition of fundamental writing skills. The program is based on sound learning principles and is devised to keep the student actively engaged throughout. It incorporates the following:

- self-pacing
- graduated levels of difficulty
- distributed practice
- immediate feedback
- overlearning
- teaching of generalizations where applicable
- selections based on adult interests

Power English is founded on the principle of overlearning, which fosters enduring retention of information and skills. Overlearning occurs when students continue practicing a skill even after they think they have learned it. In every chapter and book in the *Power English* series, through a variety of formats, students exercise skills they have learned in previous chapters and books.

The structure of the *Power English* series makes it versatile. It can be used in conventional classroom settings, in tutorial situations and clinics, or by students who work independently.

CHAPTER ONE

CAPITALIZING (TITLES OF POEMS)

Read the following:

"Chicago" is a poem by Carl Sandburg.
"Ode to the West Wind" is a poem by Percy B. Shelley.
Another poem is "He Is My Love."

Did you notice?

Most words in the titles of poems begin with capital letters.
Important small words in titles begin with capital letters, for example,
Is and **My**.

Do you remember?

The first word of a title begins with a capital letter.
Small words such as **a**, **an**, **at**, **in**, **to**, and **the** begin with small letters.

Did you know?

Quotation marks (" ") go around the title of a poem.

Try it out.

Write the following sentences over. Capitalize correctly. Remember to put
quotation marks around poem titles.

1. "to a waterfowl" is a poem by william c. bryant.

   _____

2. "when i was one-and-twenty" is a poem by a. e. housman.

   _____

3. "the road not taken" was written by robert frost.

   _____

4. "meeting at night" is a poem by robert browning.

   _____

5. "go and catch a falling star" is a poem by john donne.

   _____

STOP CHECK ANSWERS ON PAGE 137.

THE COMPLETE SUBJECT OF A SENTENCE

Read the following:

The complete subject in each sentence is underlined.

<u>Sharon</u> swims very well.

<u>Mario and I</u> love to fish.

<u>The dogs and cats</u> are running in packs.

<u>The pretty woman and the handsome man</u> are married.

Did you notice?

A complete subject can be made up of only one word—either a noun or a pronoun.

A complete subject can be made up of several nouns or pronouns or both.

A complete subject can include words that go with nouns and pronouns.

Try it out.

Draw a line under the complete subject in each sentence.

1. Chuck, Mike, and I are going camping.

2. Mrs. Moran refuses to speak to us.

3. The men, women, and children enjoyed the picnic.

4. Mr. St. Cloud and Mr. Burns went to Washington.

5. The train stopped at the wrong station.

6. A young child and her brother spilled their milk.

7. A man and child were hurt.

8. The storekeeper and a customer were robbed by a masked man.

9. The masked man had a gun and a dog.

10. The gun and dog frightened the storekeeper.

STOP CHECK ANSWERS ON PAGE 137.

SIMPLE SUBJECTS IN SENTENCES

Read the following:

<u>Jamal</u> had wanted to go to college.
His <u>parents</u> planned on it.
<u>He</u> was suspended from high school after some trouble.

Did you notice?

In those sentences nouns and pronouns are underlined.
They are the nouns and pronouns in the complete subject of each sentence.

Did you know?

One noun or pronoun in a complete subject is called the **simple subject.**

Try it out.

Fill in each blank with a subject from the list. Each sentence must make sense. A subject may be used once only.

SUBJECT LIST

apes	cats	Diane	dogs	I
lions	mother	Robert	tigers	We

1. My _____ takes care of sick animals.

2. _____ and _____ are tame animals.

3. _____, _____, and _____ are wild animals.

4. _____, _____, and _____ are animal lovers.

5. _____ help our mother take care of the animals.

STOP CHECK ANSWERS ON PAGE 137.

RECOGNIZING SENTENCES

Read the following:

There is a check by each of the sentences.

✓ Go.

  Around the corner.

  The children at the park.

✓ A bird flew into my house.

  The nasty person.

Do you remember?

A sentence has two parts.

The complete subject is the naming part of a sentence.

In commands, the complete subject, **you**, is usually not written.

The predicate is the action part of a sentence.

Try it out.

Put a check (✓) by each of the sentences.

☐ **1.** Don't play there.

☐ **2.** You are the one in charge.

☐ **3.** And in the store.

☐ **4.** Stay.

☑ **5.** He reads many books every year.

☐ **6.** Takashi can't go.

☐ **7.** The match is tomorrow.

☐ **8.** A funny man.

☐ **9.** When they show up.

☐ **10.** Try that soon.

STOP CHECK ANSWERS ON PAGE 137.

MORE THAN ONE (NOUN PLURALS)

Read the following:

one child	two children
one man	five men
one woman	six women
one goose	three geese
one mouse	four mice

Did you notice?

Some plural nouns do not end with **s** or **es**.
Those plurals are not formed according to any rule.
They must be memorized.

Do you remember?

Most plural nouns have an **s** or **es** ending.

fan	fans	box	boxes
hitch	hitches	berry	berries
dish	dishes	moss	mosses

Try it out.

Write the plural of each of the following nouns.

1. mouse _____   11. fox _____

2. child _____   12. church _____

3. foot _____   13. patch _____

4. goose _____   14. rash _____

5. tooth _____   15. tray _____

6. bag _____   16. bunny _____

7. tax _____   17. cherry _____

8. fly _____   18. candy _____

9. man _____   19. apple _____

10. woman _____   20. pass _____

STOP CHECK ANSWERS ON PAGE 137.

DESCRIBING WORDS (ADJECTIVES)

Read the following:

Mario is <u>shorter</u> than Dave.
Is Isabel <u>younger</u> than Jeff?
Dave is the <u>tallest</u> one here.
Isabel is the <u>finest</u> person in our group.

Did you notice?

The words **shorter**, **younger**, **tallest**, and **finest** are describing words.
Some describing words, such as **fine**, end with **e**.
When those words are used to compare, the **e** is dropped and **er** or **est** is added.

Do you remember?

Describing words with the **er** ending are used to compare two persons or things.
Describing words with the **est** ending compare more than two persons or things.

Try it out.

In the blank in each sentence, write the correct form of the describing word. Add an **er** or **est** ending, wherever necessary.

1. She is _____ than her sister. (**pretty**)

2. Kiyoko is the _____ friend I have. (**nice**)

3. Jim is a _____ person. (**happy**)

4. That is the _____ thing I have heard. (**silly**)

5. Tony is _____ than Bob. (**smart**)

6. The twins are _____ businessmen. (**honest**)

7. These workers are the _____ in the land. (**fine**)

8. Is José the _____ person you know? (**rich**)

9. The lake seems _____ today than yesterday. (**clean**)

10. This pond is _____ than it was last year. (**dirty**)

STOP CHECK ANSWERS ON PAGE 137.

ACTION WORDS (VERBS)

Read the following:

PRESENT TIME	PAST TIME	FUTURE TIME
I climb	I climbed	I will climb
You climb	You climbed	You will climb
He climbs	He climbed	He will climb
She climbs	She climbed	She will climb
It climbs	It climbed	It will climb
We climb	We climbed	We will climb
You climb	You climbed	You will climb
They climb	They climbed	They will climb
Andy climbs	Andy climbed	Andy will climb

Do you remember?

Many verbs end with **ed** when they describe an action that took place in the past.

The word **will** with a verb describes a future action.

Try it out.

In the blanks, write the past and future forms of each verb.

	PAST TIME	FUTURE TIME
1. They play	_____	_____
2. The house looks	_____	_____
3. The bread tastes	_____	_____
4. Ben tries	_____	_____
5. Alice cooks	_____	_____
6. Al and Fred joke	_____	_____
7. The players yell	_____	_____
8. You cry	_____	_____
9. I carry	_____	_____
10. I pray	_____	_____

STOP CHECK ANSWERS ON PAGE 137.

THE VERBS *DO, DOES, DID,* AND *WILL DO*

Read the following:

Joe <u>does</u> well in school.   Joe and Joan <u>do</u> well in school.
I <u>did</u> it yesterday.   We <u>did</u> that yesterday.
Ying <u>will do</u> it later.   Ying and Keung <u>will do</u> it later.

Do you remember?

The words **do** and **does** describe action in the present.
Does describes the action of one person or thing in the present.
Do describes the action of more than one person or thing in the present.
The word **did** describes action in the past.
The word **will** goes with **do** to describe future action.

Try it out.

Fill in each blank with **do**, **does**, **did**, or **will do**.

1. I cannot _____ that now.

2. Who _____ such a terrible thing yesterday?

3. Andrew usually _____ very good work now.

4. Jennifer and Cristina _____ a favor for us later.

5. They _____ that last month.

6. Jerry always _____ whatever he wants.

7. They _____ a good business last summer.

8. She _____ her work before.

9. The men _____ the work later.

10. The women _____ some nice things for us earlier.

STOP   CHECK ANSWERS ON PAGE 137.

9

RECOGNIZING DESCRIBING WORDS (ADVERBS)

Read the following:

Flores drives <u>slowly</u>.
Mark eats <u>quickly</u>.
Sue runs <u>swiftly</u>.
Pedro left <u>quietly</u>.

Did you notice?

The words **slowly**, **quickly**, **swiftly**, and **quietly** tell how something is or was done.
Slowly describes how Flores drives.
Quickly describes how Mark eats.
Swiftly describes how Sue runs.
Quietly describes how Pedro left.

Did you know?

Words that describe action words are called **adverbs**.
Many adverbs end with **ly**.

Try it out.

Here are ten sentences. Draw a line under each adverb.

1. On icy roads I drive <u>carefully</u>.

2. My older brothers and I spoke <u>softly</u>.

3. The pretty girl laughed <u>happily</u>.

4. The happy children shouted <u>noisily</u>.

5. The frightening dog growled <u>fiercely</u>.

6. The young child ran <u>quickly</u>.

7. The smart student answered the question <u>cleverly</u>.

8. Her child behaves <u>properly</u>.

9. The angry storekeeper shouted <u>loudly</u>.

10. My handsome groom dresses <u>beautifully</u>.

STOP CHECK ANSWERS ON PAGE 137.

RECOGNIZING DESCRIBING WORDS (ADVERBS)

Read the following:

I will see you <u>soon</u>.
Felix arrived <u>yesterday</u>.
Please come <u>tomorrow</u>.

Did you notice?

The words **soon**, **yesterday**, and **tomorrow** tell the time of an action.
Words such as **soon**, **yesterday**, and **tomorrow** are adverbs.

Do you remember?

Other adverbs tell how something is done.
Many adverbs end with **ly**.

Try it out.
Draw a line under each adverb.

1. The nice man spoke kindly.

2. Marie arrived early.

3. Frank and Mike are going to work late.

4. The small baby was crying loudly.

5. The young woman bought a dress yesterday.

6. The exciting race started promptly.

7. My handsome brother will arrive soon.

8. The dance is taking place today.

9. All my good friends will dance tonight.

10. We will go tomorrow.

STOP CHECK ANSWERS ON PAGE 137.

SHORTENING WORDS (CONTRACTIONS)

Read the following:

should not	shouldn't
is not	isn't
has not	hasn't
cannot	can't
will not	won't

Do you remember?

A number of words can join with **not** to become one word.
When a word joins with **not**, the **o** in **not** is usually omitted .
This mark (') replaces the **o**.
Cannot can be shortened to **can't**.
Will and **not** become **won't**.

Try it out.

Write the two words that are in each contraction.

1. aren't _____

2. couldn't _____

3. haven't _____

4. isn't _____

5. won't _____

Write each pair of words over as a contraction.

6. did not _____

7. should not _____

8. has not _____

9. will not _____

10. do not _____

STOP CHECK ANSWERS ON PAGE 138.

SHORTENING WORDS (CONTRACTIONS)

Read the following:

I am	I'm
you are	you're
he is	he's
she is	she's
it is	it's
we are	we're
they are	they're

Did you notice?

The pronouns **I**, **you**, **he**, **she**, **it**, **we**, and **they** can be joined with **am**, **are**, or **is**.

When a pronoun joins with **am**, **are**, or **is**, the first letter of the verb is omitted.

This mark (') replaces the omitted letter.

Do you remember?

When a word joins with **not**, the **o** in **not** is replaced by this mark (').

Try it out.

Write each pair of words over as a contraction.

1. it is _____   6. they are _____

2. could not _____   7. we are _____

3. she is _____   8. he is _____

4. cannot _____   9. has not _____

5. will not _____   10. I am _____

STOP CHECK ANSWERS ON PAGE 138.

SPELLING

Read the following:

How much do you <u>weigh</u>?
Do you know the <u>way</u> to her house?

Did you notice?

The words **weigh** and **way** sound alike.
They are spelled differently and have different meanings.

Now read the following:

In these sentences there are four sets of words like **weigh** and **way**.

He needed <u>wood</u> for his fireplace.
I <u>would</u> go if I could.

That dog's <u>tail</u> is long.
Jim told a very funny <u>tale</u>.

We <u>rode</u> all night.
The <u>road</u> was slippery.

It is not <u>fair</u> to take everything.
I do not have bus <u>fare</u>.

Try it out.

Write the correct word in each blank.

1. Please tell us a good _____. (**tail—tale**)

2. Who _____ with you yesterday? (**road—rode**)

3. Help Steve chop the _____. (**would—wood**)

4. I do not _____ so much. (**weigh—way**)

5. Mohammed does not have the plane _____. (**fair—fare**)

6. The child stepped on the cat's _____. (**tail—tale**)

7. No one _____ help the poor woman. (**would—wood**)

8. Mr. Deacon did not know the _____. (**weigh—way**)

9. The _____ was not clearly marked. (**rode—road**)

10. The workers felt their foreman was not _____. (**fare—fair**)

STOP CHECK ANSWERS ON PAGE 138.

ALPHABETIZING

Try it out.

Write the following groups of words over in alphabetical order. Put commas between the words in the lists you write.

1. cave, can, cake, came, case, cape, cat, call, cart

2. devil, deck, dew, desert, den, deep, depth, debt, deal

3. month, moth, more, move, mole, most, model, mommy, mouth

4. fan, faint, far, fat, fame, face, fade, fall, fake

5. saw, sail, sag, sat, same, sap, sane, save, safe

STOP CHECK ANSWERS ON PAGE 138.

CAPITALIZING (TITLES OF POEMS)

Write the following sentences over. Capitalize correctly. Remember to put quotation marks around poem titles.

1. i enjoyed reading the poem "a man and his dog."

   _____

2. the poem "she broke my heart" is very sad.

   _____

3. my sister wrote the poem "life can be difficult."

   _____

4. i like funny poems like "my upside down life."

   _____

5. "blowing bubbles at the world" is also very funny.

   _____

THE COMPLETE SUBJECT OF A SENTENCE

Draw a line under the complete subject in each sentence.

1. Tara, Carol, Matsue, and I are going to a movie.
2. My pets like my parents better than me.
3. My boss, his wife, and their children are coming to dinner.
4. Two strange-looking men walked into the store.
5. My older sister and younger brother do not read well.

RECOGNIZING SENTENCES

Put a check (√) by each of the sentences.

☐ 1. The large dog and the small child.

☐ 2. Go immediately.

GO ON TO THE NEXT PAGE

☐ **3.** They looked funny.

☐ **4.** My father and mother.

☐ **5.** Some people running.

MORE THAN ONE (NOUN PLURALS)

Write the plural of each of the following nouns.

1. cookie	_____	**6.** child	_____
2. goose	_____	**7.** man	_____
3. woman	_____	**8.** foot	_____
4. tooth	_____	**9.** mouse	_____
5. baby	_____	**10.** lady	_____

DESCRIBING WORDS (ADJECTIVES)

In each sentence, find the describing word, or adjective, that is used to compare. In the blank, write the describing word over correctly. Add the **er** or **est** ending.

1. My pets are noisy than my friend's pets. _____

2. That is the silly thing I have ever heard. _____

3. That dog is the dumb I have ever seen. _____

4. My dog is smart than yours. _____

5. She is the nice person I know. _____

ACTION WORDS (VERBS)

In the blanks, write the past and future forms of each verb.

	PAST TIME	FUTURE TIME
1. I jump	_____	_____
2. The lady looks	_____	_____
3. The bird lands	_____	_____
4. Edith bakes	_____	_____
5. Gary works	_____	_____

ON TO THE NEXT PAGE

THE VERBS *DO, DOES, DID,* AND *WILL DO*
Fill in each blank with **do**, **does**, **did**, or **will do**.

1. Please _____ this for me.

2. He _____ it next week.

3. We _____ that before.

4. They always _____ nice things for people.

5. Florio and Marisa _____ that already.

RECOGNIZING DESCRIBING WORDS (ADVERBS)
Draw a line under each adverb.

1. A large black car swerved toward our bus today.

2. Our frightened driver stopped carefully.

3. A large brown dog suddenly jumped onto our bus.

4. The people on the bus screamed loudly.

5. A police car rushed to the scene quickly.

6. The dog was waiting quietly.

7. We waited anxiously.

8. Everyone chatted noisily.

9. The police captured the dog immediately.

10. The bus driver opened the door slowly.

SHORTENING WORDS (CONTRACTIONS)
Write each pair of words over as a contraction.

1. are not _____

2. is not _____

3. have not _____

4. they are _____

5. she is _____

6. will not _____

7. cannot _____

8. I am _____

9. we are _____

10. you are _____

GO ON TO THE NEXT PAGE

SPELLING

These sentences have misspelled words. They do not make sense. Write each sentence over so that it makes sense. Spell each word correctly.

1. I have the fair two go to the fare.

_____

2. Wood you tell the child a tail?

_____

3. They road on the rode two get too my house.

_____

4. That wood not be fare.

_____

5. Which is the weigh two your house?

_____

ALPHABETIZING

Write the following names in alphabetical order. Put commas between the names in the list you write.

1. Cook, Forbes, Gates, Fermes, Fellini, Foster, Colby, Combs

_____

2. Dean, Dermo, Deitz, Demo, Drake, Drell, Dromer, Delgado

_____

3. Katz, Karro, Kant, Kramer, Kent, Krell, Kashiwada, Kepler

_____

4. Sanchez, Sardo, Samson, Sato, Sappo, Sasso, Sago, Saber

_____

5. Anderson, Acker, Adler, Amber, Arrio, Alvarez, Ace, Able

_____

STOP CHECK ANSWERS BEGINNING ON PAGE 138.

Count how many items you answered correctly in each **Section** of the Chapter One Review. Write your score per section in the **My Scores** column. If all of your section scores are as high as the **Good Scores**, go on to Chapter Two. If any of your section scores are lower than the **Good Scores**, study the lessons on the assigned **Review Pages** again before you go on to Chapter Two.

Section	Good Scores	My Scores	Review Pages
Capitalizing (Titles of Poems)	4 or 5		2
The Complete Subject of a Sentence	4 or 5		3
Recognizing Sentences	4 or 5		5
More Than One (Noun Plurals)	8, 9, or 10		6
Describing Words (Adjectives)	4 or 5		7
Action Words (Verbs)	4 or 5		8
The Verbs **Do**, **Does**, **Did**, and **Will Do**	4 or 5		9
Recognizing Describing Words (Adverbs)	8, 9, or 10		10–11
Shortening Words (Contractions)	8, 9, or 10		12–13
Spelling	4 or 5		14
Alphabetizing	4 or 5		15

CHAPTER TWO

CAPITALIZING (TITLES OF POEMS AND STORIES)

Read the following:

"Fog" is a poem.
Another poem is "The Night Will Never Stay."
"The Night Is Young" is a short story.
Another short story is "The Monkey's Paw."
"Little Red Riding Hood" is also a short story.

Do you remember?

Most words in titles of poems and short stories begin with capital letters.
The first word of a title begins with a capital letter.
Small words like **will**, **is**, and **red** begin with capital letters.
Small words like **a**, **an**, **and**, **for**, **in**, **on**, **to**, and **the** begin with small letters.

Try it out.

Write the following sentences over. Capitalize correctly. Remember to put quotation marks around poem and short story titles and to underline book titles.

1. armin and i read "my life is a bowl of jelly" for the class.

   _____

2. mr. and mrs. blake wrote the short story "many loves."

   _____

3. my favorite book is how to fix your house.

   _____

4. franco's child likes the book the cat in the hat.

   _____

5. my sister has read "my life is just a dream" twice.

   _____

STOP CHECK ANSWERS ON PAGE 139.

COMPOUND SUBJECTS IN SENTENCES

Read the following:

COMPLETE SUBJECT	PREDICATE
Typewriters and adding machines	are outdated.
Word processors and calculators	work more efficiently.

Did you notice?

There are two nouns in each of the complete subjects.
Because the subjects name more than one thing, the verbs in the predicates are plural.

Did you know?

At least one noun or pronoun is part of the complete subject of any sentence.
Some sentences have two or more nouns and pronouns in the complete subject.
Those sentences have **compound subjects**.

Try it out.

Find the words from Group Two, the predicate, that go with each complete subject from Group One. Write the letter in the blank.

GROUP ONE (COMPLETE SUBJECT)	GROUP TWO (PREDICATE)
_e_ 1. Coffee and tea	**a.** are comic book heroes.
_h_ 2. Cereal and eggs	**b.** are needed for plants.
_c_ 3. The lion and its trainer	**c.** perform in a cage.
___ 4. Dinosaurs and flying reptiles	**d.** are wild animals.
___ 5. Superman and Batman	**e.** are common breakfast drinks.
___ 6. Sun and water	**f.** are citrus fruits.
___ 7. The bus and train	**g.** no longer exist.
___ 8. Pepper and garlic	**h.** are typical breakfast foods.
___ 9. Lions and tigers	**i.** are ways to get to work.
_f_ 10. Oranges and lemons	**j.** make food taste better.

STOP CHECK ANSWERS ON PAGE 139.

COMPOUND VERBS IN SENTENCES

Read the following:

Sharee sings and dances.

The children run and play.

Dick draws, spells, and writes well.

Did you notice?

Each sentence has two or more verbs.

Each verb in a sentence goes with the subject.

Did you know?

At least one verb is part of the predicate of any sentence.

Some sentences have two or more verbs in the predicate.

Those sentences have **compound verbs**.

Try it out.

Draw lines under the verbs in each sentence.

1. At the beach, the man chased the dog and grabbed it.

2. The dog barked and snapped at the man.

3. Some people stopped and watched.

4. The man talked softly to the dog and stroked it.

5. A bird dropped from the sky and swooped down near the dog.

6. A woman opened her window and looked out.

7. The dog slumped on the ground and moaned.

8. A child tiptoed up to the dog and touched it.

9. The dog barked and frightened the child.

10. The child dashed across the beach and played with the dog.

STOP CHECK ANSWERS ON PAGE 139.

RECOGNIZING SENTENCES

Read the following:

There is a check by each of the sentences.
√ Stay away.
  The hungry children are.
√ No one is here.

Did you notice?

This is a not a sentence:
  The hungry children are.
There is a subject: **The hungry children**
There is a verb: **are**
However, the sentences does not express a complete idea. It does not make sense.

Do you remember?

A sentence has two parts, a complete subject and a predicate.
A sentence expresses a complete thought; it makes sense.

Try it out.

Put a check (√) by each of the sentences.

☐ **1.** Put that down.

☐ **2.** Who said that?

☐ **3.** The chair and the table look.

☐ **4.** My friends and their parents have.

☐ **5.** Rose, Chuck, and Anita look happy.

☐ **6.** They seem very quiet.

☐ **7.** Show me how to do that.

☐ **8.** Go.

☐ **9.** Please stay a little longer.

☐ **10.** The oven was.

STOP CHECK ANSWERS ON PAGE 139.

COMMAND SENTENCES

Read the following:

Stop.   Stop!
Run.   Run!
Move.   Move!

Do you remember?

Command sentences usually end with periods (.).
An exclamation point (!) may be used to show strong feeling.
Command sentences usually have unstated subjects.
The subject **you** is understood in most command sentences:

Stop. means **You stop**.
Run. means **You run**.
Move. means **You move**.

Try it out.

Put the correct end mark at the end of each sentence.

1. Stay

2. Halt

3. That is the best news I have ever heard

4. Come down

5. Put that down

6. Who took the tools

7. Sue is leaving now

8. Margaret is helping Frank learn to read

9. I am leaving soon

10. Please show that to me

STOP   CHECK ANSWERS ON PAGE 139.

Read the following:

The car hit the child.
It hurt the child badly.

The man was very sorry.
He did not mean to do it.

The children were playing in the street.
They did not see the car.

The car threw the child onto me.
I was very upset.

Do you remember?

Words such as **I**, **you**, **he**, **she**, **it**, **we**, and **they** are used in place of naming words.
Such words are called **pronouns**.

Try it out.

Here are pair of sentences. Fill in each blank with **I**, **you**, **he**, **she**, **it**, **we**, or **they**.

1. The car could have hit me.

   _____ was scared.

2. The hurt child is a seven-year-old girl.

   _____ is still in the hospital.

3. Her friends were very upset.

   _____ visited her in the hospital.

4. My parents and I sent her a card.

   _____ also visited her in the hospital.

5. The children do not play in the street now.

   _____ do not want to get hurt.

STOP CHECK ANSWERS ON PAGE 140.

27

THE PRONOUNS *I, YOU, HE, SHE, IT, WE,* AND *THEY*

Read the following:

The pronouns in this story are underlined.

Cheryl and Tyree are both bank tellers. <u>They</u> often have to work late. If Cheryl gets off earlier than Tyree, <u>she</u> cooks. If Tyree is earlier, <u>he</u> cooks. <u>You</u> can't find better cooperation than that.

Do you remember?

Pronouns take the place of nouns.
Pronouns are words such as **I, you, he, she, it, we** and **they**.

Try it out.

Here is a story with blanks. Fill in the blanks with **I, you, he, she, it, we,** or **they**. You will use some of the pronouns more than once.

In May of last year, my girlfriend and _____ broke up.
(1)

_____ both decided it would be for the best. Before last week,
(2)

_____ had not spoken to her or seen her. Last week, one of my
(3)

friends and _____ saw her at a party. _____ looked
(4)   (5)

very good. _____ was there with someone I know.
(6)

_____ both seemed to be having a good time. That made me feel
(7)

sick. Other people at the party were dancing and singing. _____,
(8)

too, were having a good time. _____ was the only one who was
(9)

not having a good time. I knew then that _____ was jealous.
(10)

STOP   CHECK ANSWERS ON PAGE 140.

THE VERBS *HAS, HAVE, HAD,* AND *WILL HAVE*

Read the following:

Eric <u>has</u> a good job.   Hiroko and Eric <u>have</u> good jobs.
Laura <u>had</u> a baby last year.   They <u>had</u> a baby last year.
Flo <u>will have</u> a job soon.   Flo and Al <u>will have</u> a job soon.

Do you remember?

The words **has** and **have** describe action in the present.
Has describes the action of one person or thing in the present.
Have describes the action of **I**, **you**, or more than one other person or thing in the present.
The word **had** describes action in the past.
The word **will** goes with **have** to describe future action.

Try it out.

Fill in each blank with **had**, **has**, **have**, or **will have**.

1. I _____ no job after tomorrow.

2. My boss and I _____ a fight yesterday.

3. I _____ a problem now.

4. My boss _____ a terrible temper.

5. He also _____ a lot of power.

6. I _____ no money coming in after tomorrow.

7. My wife _____ no job.

8. We _____ another child soon.

9. I _____ a lot of anger in me yesterday.

10. My wife and children still _____ hope.

STOP   CHECK ANSWERS ON PAGE 140.

THE VERBS *SEE, SEES, SAW,* AND *WILL SEE*

Read the following:

My boss <u>sees</u> everything.   My bosses <u>see</u> everything.
The dog <u>saw</u> her.   The dogs <u>saw</u> her.
My teacher <u>will see</u> me soon.   My teachers <u>will see</u> me soon.

Did you notice?

The words **see** and **sees** describe action in the present.
Sees describes the action of one person or thing in the present.
See describes the action of more than one person or thing in the present.
The word **saw** describes action in the past.
The word **will** goes with **see** to describe future action.

Try it out.

Fill in each blank with **see**, **sees**, **saw**, or **will see**.

1. Emily _____ an accident last week.

2. Linda and Michael _____ another accident just before.

3. Mrs. Murphy _____ very well these days.

4. Her husband cannot _____ without his glasses.

5. Dr. Peterson _____ him tomorrow.

6. Doctors often _____ many sad things.

7. A while ago Mr. and Mrs. Florio _____ a man dash in front of a truck.

8. The truck driver _____ the man in time.

9. Many people _____ another near-accident.

10. The driver _____ that person in time, too.

STOP   CHECK ANSWERS ON PAGE 140.

THE VERBS SEE, SEES, SAW, AND WILL SEE

Read the following:

PRESENT TIME	PAST TIME	FUTURE TIME
I see.	I saw.	I will see.
You see.	You saw.	You will see.
He sees.	He saw.	He will see.
She sees.	She saw.	She will see.
It sees.	It saw.	It will see.
We see.	We saw.	We will see.
They see.	They saw.	They will see.

Did you notice?

The words **see** and **sees** describe action in the present.
See goes with the pronouns **I**, **you**, **we**, and **they**.
Sees goes with the pronouns **he**, **she**, and **it**.
The word **saw** describes action in the past.
The words **will see** describe future action.

Try it out.

Fill in each blank with **see**, **sees**, **saw**, or **will see**.

1. He _____ you in a minute.

2. I _____ it now.

3. They _____ him yesterday.

4. She _____ very well with her new glasses now.

5. Yes, I _____ my girlfriend standing there before.

6. We _____ them a short time ago.

7. I _____ Sancho tomorrow.

8. You _____ us later.

9. He _____ me yesterday.

10. They _____ their friends soon.

STOP CHECK ANSWERS ON PAGE 140.

SHORTENING WORDS (CONTRACTIONS)

Read the following:

I will	I'll
you will	you'll
he will	he'll
she will	she'll
it will	it'll
we will	we'll
they will	they'll

The pronouns **I**, **you**, **he**, **she**, **it**, **we**, and **they** can be joined with **will**.
When a pronoun joins with **will**, the first two letters, **wi**, are omitted.
This mark (') replaces the omitted letters.

Do you remember?

The word **will** is used with verbs when they describe future action.
Pronouns can be joined with **am**, **are**, and **is**.
Many words can be joined with **not**.

Try it out.

Write each pair of words as a contraction.

1. I am _____
2. he is _____
3. I will _____
4. she will _____
5. is not _____
6. could not _____
7. they will _____
8. cannot _____
9. will not _____
10. we will _____

11. should not _____
12. they are _____
13. would not _____
14. he will _____
15. you will _____
16. has not _____
17. have not _____
18. are not _____
19. it is _____
20. did not _____

STOP CHECK ANSWERS ON PAGE 140.

THE WORDS *A* AND *AN*

Do you remember?

The word **an** goes before words that begin with a vowel sound.
The word **a** goes before words that begin with a consonant sound.
The word **a** goes before **union** and **usual** and other words that begin with a **y** sound.

Try it out.

Put **a** or **an** before each of the following.

1. _____ unusual day   5. _____ icy street   9. _____ bald man

2. _____ umbrella   6. _____ ant   10. _____ unit price

3. _____ open door   7. _____ upper floor

4. _____ pear   8. _____ underground safe

STOP   CHECK ANSWERS ON PAGE 140.

SPELLING

Read the following:

I am a <u>fair</u> person.
I need train <u>fare</u>.

Show her the <u>way</u> to the store.
I <u>weigh</u> too much.

Who <u>would</u> do that?
The <u>wood</u> is wet.

The father <u>read</u> a book to his child.
His book has a <u>red</u> cover.

I do not <u>know</u> her.
<u>No</u>, I will not go.

Do you remember?

Many words that sound alike are spelled differently and have different meanings.

Try it out.

These sentences have misspelled words. They do not make sense. Write each sentence over so that it makes sense. Spell each word correctly.

1. She wood not go that weigh.

   _____

2. I red a good book an our ago, two.

   _____

3. You are not going the write weigh to her house.

   _____

4. To be fare, the man gave each child bus fair.

   _____

5. Know, I do not no the write person for the job.

   _____

STOP CHECK ANSWERS ON PAGE 140.

ALPHABETIZING

Try it out.

Write the following groups of words over in alphabetical order. Put commas between the words in the lists you write.

1. pretty, pack, party, pull, pride, push, pad, pure, paid, put, page, peace, pet, past, pen

   _____

   _____

2. sore, saw, some, sat, soap, set, sell, seam, sum, sue, seem, sold, sit, sure, suit

   _____

   _____

3. tear, tore, treat, tar, toe, too, top, try, trail, tick, tub, tour, trip, teeth, tip

   _____

   _____

GO ON TO THE NEXT PAGE

4. wear, were, was, wall, where, whack, well, wait, while, water, won, witch, win, why, wet

_____

_____

5. apple, am, ate, are, again, an, ape, another, arrest, ant, ace, ask, aunt, add, after

_____

_____

STOP CHECK ANSWERS ON PAGE 140.

CAPITALIZING (TITLES OF POEMS AND STORIES)

Write the following sentences over. Capitalize correctly. Remember to put quotation marks around poem and short story titles and to underline book titles.

1. the story "the canary flew the coop" is not about a bird.

_____

2. "making duck soup" is a silly story.

_____

3. herb and sara wrote the story "help is on the way."

_____

4. how to fix everything is the best book i own.

_____

5. i like the poem "i need a break."

_____

COMPOUND SUBJECTS IN SENTENCES

Find the words from Group Two, the predicate, that go with each complete subject from Group One. Write the letter in the blank.

GROUP ONE (COMPLETE SUBJECT)

____ 1. An evil man and his wife

_A_ 2. They

_A_ 3. The child

____ 4. The parents and police

____ 5. The call

GROUP TWO (PREDICATE)

a. was only three months old.

b. stole a child from his parents.

c. never came.

d. wanted to sell the child to a childless couple.

e. waited for a phone call.

GO ON TO THE NEXT PAGE

COMPOUND VERBS IN SENTENCES
Draw a line under each verb in each sentence.

1. The parents cried and begged for help.

2. They appeared on TV and talked to millions of people about their child.

3. A woman saw the TV show and phoned the police.

4. The police jumped into their cars and rushed to her house.

5. At the house they rescued the baby and returned him to his parents.

RECOGNIZING SENTENCES
Put a check (√) by each of the sentences.

☐ 1. Help is on the way.

☐ 2. Rush there immediately.

☐ 3. Into the room and around there.

☐ 4. Harold and Yolanda are.

☐ 5. The interesting people and their friends.

COMMAND SENTENCES
Put the correct end mark at the end of each sentence.

1. Find that killer immediately

2. Please hold this for me

3. Why did she do it

4. You should not leave your baby alone outside

5. Go

THE PRONOUNS *I, YOU, HE, SHE, IT, WE,* AND *THEY*
Fill in each blank with **I, you, he, she, it, we,** or **they**.

1. The parents screamed with joy.

   _____ were overjoyed to get their baby back.

2. The family pet was happy to see the baby.

   _____ meowed and meowed.

GO ON TO THE NEXT PAGE

3. My friends and I read about it.

   _____ were happy, too.

4. The woman had found the baby on her doorstep.

   _____ called the police.

5. The story made me feel good.

   _____ like happy endings.

THE PRONOUNS *I, YOU, HE, SHE, IT, WE,* AND *THEY*

Fill in each blank with **I**, **you**, **he**, **she**, **it**, **we**, or **they**. You will use some of the pronouns more than once.

_____ was the only child in my family. My parents both came
(1)

from very large families. _____ had many brothers and sisters.
(2)

My parents wanted more children. _____ couldn't have any more.
(3)

Even today, my parents and _____ have lots of fun together.
(4)

_____ like many of the same things.
(5)

THE VERBS *HAS, HAVE, HAD,* AND *WILL HAVE*

Fill in each blank with **has**, **have**, **had**, or **will have**.

1. He _____ a nice tan now.

2. Arturo _____ a better tan last summer.

3. I _____ my tooth out tomorrow.

4. _____ that ready for me.

5. She _____ a headache an hour ago.

GO ON TO THE NEXT PAGE

THE VERBS *SEE, SEES, SAW,* AND *WILL SEE*

Fill in each blank with **see**, **sees**, **saw**, or **will see**.

1. The Roths _____ them at a party yesterday.

2. I _____ them last week.

3. He _____ his former girlfriend later.

4. Joanne _____ very well now.

5. Jerry _____ her just a while ago.

6. Bill and Alice _____ each other a lot now.

7. The dog _____ me in its yard earlier.

8. I _____ poorly with my old glasses now.

9. Camille and I _____ Jennifer and Kenji in an hour.

10. Please, _____ me for a moment.

SHORTENING WORDS (CONTRACTIONS)

Write each pair of words as a contraction.

1. I will _____   6. cannot _____

2. they will _____   7. she is _____

3. we are _____   8. he will _____

4. you will _____   9. has not _____

5. I am _____   10. we will _____

THE WORDS *A* AND *AN*

Put **a** or **an** before each of the following.

1. _____ union worker   6. _____ used car

2. _____ usual day   7. _____ young man

3. _____ honest person   8. _____ pink dress

4. _____ dark street   9. _____ opera

5. _____ green umbrella   10. _____ Easter bunny

GO ON TO THE NEXT PAGE

SPELLING

Put the correct word in each blank.

1. I _____ him a story a moment ago. (**red—read**)

2. We need _____ for the fireplace. (**would—wood**)

3. _____ you do it now, please? (**Would—Wood**)

4. _____ , I do not _____ him. (**Know—No**)

5. The _____ on the train is not _____ . (**fare—fair**)

ALPHABETIZING

Write the following groups of words over in alphabetical order. Put commas between the words in the lists you write.

1. sew, set, sack, sell, send, serious, September, seven, search

   _____

2. cafe, car, cab, came, cage, cape, cane, call, cake

   _____

3. green, give, gas, grass, grim, gave, gone, girl, grow

   _____

4. try, tail, this, trip, tale, train, these, tree, that

   _____

5. bar, bail, baby, bag, bank, base, bad, back, bat

   _____

STOP CHECK YOUR ANSWERS BEGINNING ON PAGE 140.

Count how many items you answered correctly in each **Section** of the Chapter Two Review. Write your score per section in the **My Scores** column. If all of your section scores are as high as the **Good Scores**, go on to Chapter Three. If any of your section scores are lower than the **Good Scores**, study the lessons on the assigned **Review Pages** again before you go on to Chapter Three.

Section	Good Scores	My Scores	Review Pages
Capitalizing (Titles of Poems and Stories)	4 or 5		22
Compound Subjects in Sentences	4 or 5		23
Compound Verbs in Sentences	4 or 5		24
Recognizing Sentences	4 or 5		25
Command Sentences	4 or 5		26
The Pronouns **I**, **You**, **He**, **She**, **It**, **We**, and **They**	4 or 5		27–28
The Pronouns **I**, **You**, **He**, **She**, **It**, **We**, and **They**	4 or 5		27–28
The Verbs **Has**, **Have**, **Had**, and **Will Have**	4 or 5		29
The Verbs **See**, **Sees**, **Saw**, and **Will See**	8, 9, or 10		30–31
Shortening Words (Contractions)	8, 9, or 10		32
The Words **A** and **An**	8, 9, or 10		33
Spelling	4 or 5		34
Alphabetizing	4 or 5		35–36

CHAPTER THREE

CAPITALIZING (NAMES OF COUNTRIES)

Read the following:

Egypt
England
Hong Kong
Italy
Spain
United States of America

Did you notice?

Names of countries begin with capital letters.

Do you remember?

The following begin with capital letters:
the first words in sentences
people's names and initials
the names of months

Try it out.

Write the following sentences over. Capitalize correctly.

1. clara left poland to come to the united states of america.

_____

_____

2. harry s. white left austria in june to come to america.

_____

_____

3. mrs. i. longo has lived in iran, china, japan, and france.

_____

_____

GO ON TO THE NEXT PAGE

4. the cramers and i traveled to canada, alaska, and italy.

_____

_____

5. ellen tabrizi traveled to russia, ireland, germany, and spain.

_____

_____

STOP CHECK ANSWERS ON PAGE 141.

SENTENCE PARTS

Try it out.

Find the words from Group Two, the predicate, that go with each complete subject from Group One. Write the letter in the blank.

GROUP ONE (COMPLETE SUBJECT)	GROUP TWO (PREDICATE)
____ 1. Jake	a. are not very friendly to Jake.
____ 2. My boss	b. am the only one talking to him.
____ 3. The other workers	c. invited Jake's wife to our home.
____ 4. I	d. just hired Jake last week.
____ 5. Which person	e. had a good time at our house.
____ 6. My wife	f. is a new worker.
____ 7. His wife	g. will help him?
____ 8. It	h. should ignore anyone.
____ 9. No one	i. is difficult enough.
____ 10. Life	j. is not nice to be mean.

STOP CHECK ANSWERS ON PAGE 142.

SHORTENING SENTENCES WITH COMMAS

Read the following:

The screaming people and the crying children and the shouting policemen frightened me.

Now read the following:

The screaming people, the crying children, and the shouting policemen frightened me.

Did you notice?

In the sentence there are more than two nouns in the complete subject.

Commas (,) can be used to shorten sentences.

The comma replaces **and**—except for the last **and**—in the list of nouns.

There is no comma after the last noun in the complete subject.

Try it out.

Write the following sentences over. Shorten them by using commas.

1. All my aunts and uncles and cousins and grandparents visited me last week.

   _____

2. History and geography and arithmetic are my favorite topics.

   _____

3. The workers and their families and their bosses are at a picnic.

   _____

4. The birds and the bees and the flowers tell me it is spring.

   _____

5. The monkeys and the lions and the tigers and the birds cannot be fed by zoo visitors.

   _____

STOP CHECK ANSWERS ON PAGE 142.

SHORTENING SENTENCES WITH COMMAS

Try it out.

Write the following sentences over. Shorten them by using commas.

1. Turkey and chicken and fish are what my doctor wants me to eat.

   _____

2. Ms. Rivera and Mr. Jordan and Mrs. James are in business together.

   _____

3. The cake and the ice cream and the cookies and the candy you eat are high in sugar and fat.

   _____

4. The grapefruits and the oranges and the lemons and the limes were damaged in shipment.

   _____

5. Jerry and Tran and Adam and Derrick work together.

   _____

STOP CHECK ANSWERS ON PAGE 142.

48

WORD ORDER IN SENTENCES AND COMMAS

Read the following:

And Antoine Cheryl Scott traveling in the United States are.

Did you notice?

The words do not mean anything.
They do not make a sentence.
They should say this:

Antoine, Cheryl, and Scott are traveling in the United States.

Do you remember?

There should be commas between three or more nouns in a complete subject.
The word **and** goes before the last noun in the list.

Try it out.

Use the following groups of words to write sentences. Add necessary commas.

1. Men women children the and picnic at were.

   _____

2. Into woods mothers fathers children dogs ran and the.

   _____

3. Heard large everyone a growl.

   _____

4. Men frightened women were children dogs the and.

   _____

5. Bear they them saw a toward coming.

   _____

STOP CHECK ANSWERS ON PAGE 142.

RECOGNIZING NAMING WORDS (NOUNS)

Read the following:

The <u>stone</u> just missed hitting <u>Liz</u> in her <u>eye</u>.
<u>Mack</u> and <u>Dave</u> build <u>houses</u>.

Did you notice?

The nouns in the sentences are underlined.
Some of the nouns name one person or thing: **stone, Liz, eye, Mack, Dave**.
One of them names more than one thing: **houses**.
The people's names begin with capital letters: **Liz, Mack, Dave**.

Do you remember?

Nouns name persons, animals, things, places, and ideas or feelings.

Try it out.

Draw a line under each of the nouns in the following short story.

Last summer Pedro and his brother Sancho went to camp. The camp was in the country. Pedro was a lifeguard. His brother worked as his helper. There were many young children at the camp. During the year, the children all lived in the city. The children had never been out of the city. This was the first time they were in the country.

The camp had a small farm and garden. Some children had never seen a cow or a chicken. The children loved working in the garden. They also loved feeding the animals. Pedro, his brother, and all the children had a good time at camp.

STOP CHECK ANSWERS ON PAGE 142.

THE VERBS *GO, GOES, WENT,* AND *WILL GO*

Read the following:

The child <u>goes</u> to school.   The children <u>go</u> to school.
Mr. Brown <u>went</u> to work.   The Browns <u>went</u> to work.
Miss Shapiro <u>will go</u> out.   The Shapiros <u>will go</u> out.

Did you notice?

The words **go** and **goes** describe action in the present.
Goes describes the action of one person or thing in the present.
Go describes the action of more than one person or thing in the present.
The word **went** describes action in the past.
The word **will**, together with **go**, describes future action.

Try it out.

Fill in each blank with **go**, **goes**, **went**, or **will go**.

1. George _____ there tomorrow.

2. Ann _____ to the bank for me every week.

3. Ben _____ to his office earlier this morning.

4. Harry and Noriko _____ to the store before.

5. Nick _____ to the gym every day now.

6. My friends _____ to the movies yesterday.

7. Don _____ to the library in a few hours.

8. The workers _____ home soon.

9. Miss Valdez _____ to work in an hour.

10. Julio and Ramon _____ to their club last weekend.

STOP   CHECK ANSWERS ON PAGE 142.

THE VERBS *GO, GOES, WENT,* AND *WILL GO*

Read the following:

PRESENT TIME	PAST TIME	FUTURE TIME
I go.	I went.	I will go.
You go.	You went.	You will go.
She goes.	She went.	She will go.
He goes.	He went.	He will go.
It goes.	It went.	It will go.
We go.	We went.	We will go.
They go.	They went.	They will go.

Did you notice?

The words **go** and **goes** describe action in the present.
Go is used with the pronouns **I**, **you**, **we**, and **they**.
Goes is used with the pronouns **he**, **she**, and **it**.
The word **went** describes action in the past.
The words **will go** describe future action.

Try it out.

Fill in each blank with **go**, **goes**, **went**, or **will go**.

1. They _____ tomorrow.

2. It _____ well for him earlier.

3. We _____ to the beach yesterday.

4. You _____ to the movies every week now.

5. He _____ out of town an hour ago.

6. I _____ to my friend's party last night.

7. She _____ to the store every day.

8. We _____ to the bowling alley last week.

9. They _____ swimming shortly.

10. It _____ badly for him tomorrow.

STOP CHECK ANSWERS ON PAGE 142.

DESCRIBING WORDS (ADVERBS)

Read the following:

The silly child stood <u>there</u>.   The teacher put the papers <u>away</u>.
We remained <u>here</u>.

Did you notice?

The words **there**, **here**, and **away** tell where the action took place.

Did you know?

There are other words that tell where an action takes place: **inside**, **outside**, **below**, **above**, and **down**.
Words that tell where something takes place are **adverbs**.

Do you remember?

Words that tell when or how an action takes place are also adverbs.

Try it out.

Fill in each blank with an adverb from the following list. Use each adverb **only once**.

ADVERB LIST

away	here	inside	late	nearby
now	outside	suddenly	tomorrow	yesterday

1. My aunt will arrive in the early afternoon _____ .

2. Her plane always arrives _____ .

3. Then it takes a long time to bring the luggage _____ .

4. They once left her luggage _____ in the rain.

5. My best friend went home in the morning _____ .

6. I was sorry to see him go _____ .

7. He does not live _____ .

8. My aunt will have his room _____ .

9. She likes to stay _____ with us.

10. Her husband died _____ last year.

STOP   CHECK ANSWERS ON PAGE 142.

THE WORDS *A* AND *AN*

Read the following:

a happy child   an hour   an x-ray

Do you remember?

The word **an** goes before words that begin with a vowel sound.
The word **a** goes before words that begin with a consonant sound.
An goes before the words **hour** and **x-ray** because they begin with vowel sounds.

Try it out.

Put **a** or **an** before each of the following.

1. _____ hand

2. _____ house

3. _____ hourglass

4. _____ union leader

5. _____ hungry worker

6. _____ hourly wage

7. _____ history lesson

8. _____ x-ray machine

9. _____ bottle

10. _____ ape

11. _____ sick person

12. _____ healthy animal

13. _____ unmade bed

14. _____ farmer

15. _____ idea

16. _____ mouse

17. _____ open door

18. _____ leaf

19. _____ chair

20. _____ hot tub

STOP   CHECK ANSWERS ON PAGE 142.

WRITING ADDRESSES

Read the following:

Jack Silvers lives in Detroit, Michigan.
Barry Hodges lives in New York, New York.
Mario Gallo lives in Chicago, Illinois.

Did you notice?

Each sentence has a city and state.
There is a comma between the city and the state.
The comma separates the city from the state.

Try it out.

Write each of the following sentences over. Add necessary commas.

1. José moved to Buffalo New York.

   _____

2. Sandy has a new job in Reno Nevada.

   _____

3. My parents live in Columbus Ohio.

   _____

4. Are you going to Seattle Washington?

   _____

5. Is your friend in Trenton New Jersey?

   _____

6. My girlfriend lives in Little Rock Arkansas.

   _____

GO ON TO THE NEXT PAGE

7. Her grandparents recently moved to Miami Florida.

_____

8. Nader lives in Atlanta Georgia.

_____

9. Amy now lives in San Francisco California.

_____

10. Who recently left for Tulsa Oklahoma?

_____

STOP CHECK ANSWERS ON PAGE 143.

WRITING THE TIME OF DAY

Read the following:

The train will arrive at 9:00 A.M.
Chai is leaving at 10:30 P.M. tomorrow.
I can't make it at 1:45 P.M. on Monday.

Did you notice?

There is a colon (:) between the hour and the minutes in the time. The part of the day, **A.M.** or **P.M.**, is written with capital letters followed by periods.

Try it out.

Write the following times correctly.

1. 1225 pm _____

2. 925 am _____

3. 1100 am _____

4. 645 pm _____

5. 1215 am _____

6. 800 pm _____

7. 345 am _____

8. 1000 pm _____

9. 230 am _____

10. 445 pm _____

STOP CHECK ANSWERS ON PAGE 143.

SPELLING

Read the following:

| can | canned | stop | stopped |
| bat | batted | drip | dripped |

Did you notice?

These words each have one vowel: **can, bat, stop, drip**.
One consonant follows the vowel in each word.
When an **ed** ending is added to such a word, the final consonant is doubled.

Now read the following:

In each of the following words, there are two vowels or two final consonants.
No change is made when the **ed** ending is added.

| corn | corned | stoop | stooped |
| bait | baited | drill | drilled |

Try it out.

Add the **ed** ending to each of the following words. Double the final consonant, if necessary.

1. fit _____
2. pin _____
3. shop _____
4. boil _____
5. fail _____
6. drop _____
7. pet _____
8. cook _____
9. mail _____
10. fan _____

11. stop _____
12. tan _____
13. trap _____
14. step _____
15. steam _____
16. look _____
17. chop _____
18. broil _____
19. chat _____
20. fill _____

STOP CHECK ANSWERS ON PAGE 143.

58

ALPHABETIZING

Read the following:

ace   act   back   bad   bar   bay   cab   can
These words are in the order of the alphabet.

Try it out.

Here are forty-eight words. Write them in alphabetical order.

sure	were	ant	night	queen	why	pan	sun
war	seem	wax	only	cave	sorry	quick	zoo
near	one	x-ray	man	while	fat	up	jail
won	name	run	cute	call	son	girl	cup
can	cure	soap	what	bear	rich	wake	so
when	care	net	cape	set	home	cake	day

1. _____
2. _____
3. _____
4. _____
5. _____
6. _____
7. _____
8. _____
9. _____
10. _____
11. _____
12. _____
13. _____
14. _____
15. _____
16. _____

17. _____
18. _____
19. _____
20. _____
21. _____
22. _____
23. _____
24. _____
25. _____
26. _____
27. _____
28. _____
29. _____
30. _____
31. _____
32. _____

33. _____
34. _____
35. _____
36. _____
37. _____
38. _____
39. _____
40. _____
41. _____
42. _____
43. _____
44. _____
45. _____
46. _____
47. _____
48. _____

STOP CHECK ANSWERS ON PAGE 143.

CAPITALIZING (NAMES OF COUNTRIES)

Write the following sentences over. Capitalize correctly.

1. i dream of traveling to places such as italy, spain, and greece.

   _____

2. joe and i saved for two years to visit our parents in poland.

   _____

3. i can only afford to travel to new jersey from new york.

   _____

4. andrew and i are going to france on our honeymoon.

   _____

5. sara, donna, sonia, and i are going to china next summer.

   _____

SENTENCE PARTS

Find the words from Group Two, the predicate, that go with each complete subject from Group One. Write the letter in the blank.

GROUP ONE (COMPLETE SUBJECT)	GROUP TWO (PREDICATE)
____ 1. This Christmas	**a.** am out of work.
____ 2. I	**b.** are very old.
____ 3. My children	**c.** will be a difficult one.
____ 4. My parents	**d.** will make this a good Christmas.
____ 5. Only a miracle	**e.** need many things.

GO ON TO THE NEXT PAGE

SHORTENING SENTENCES WITH COMMAS

Write the following sentences over. Shorten them by using commas.

1. The dirty coat and the sweater and the skirt need cleaning.

   _____

2. The Gerbers and the Steins and the Benders are nice people.

   _____

3. The mother and the father and the brother and the sister look alike.

   _____

4. The dog and the cat and the bird live with me.

   _____

5. The truck and the car and the van couldn't get out of the mud.

   _____

WORD ORDER IN SENTENCES AND COMMAS

Use the following groups of words to write sentences. Add necessary commas.

1. Friends I and Joanne are Marion good.

   _____

2. Fish need I buy vegetables to and fruit.

   _____

3. Year visited Charles I Michael China last and.

   _____

4. Italy and and going are I Maria Portugal Greece to.

   _____

5. Visit and I to Hawaii Bermuda would Jamaica like.

   _____

GO ON TO THE NEXT PAGE

NAMING WORDS (NOUNS)

Fill in each blank with a noun from the list. Use the word that makes the most sense in the story. Use each word **only once**.

NOUN LIST

boss	brothers	date	family	girl
house	love	parents	questions	result

I have three _____ . They love me a lot. I love them, too.
(1)

However, their _____ can be a problem. I am the youngest
(2)

_____ in our _____ . As a _____ they all try
(3)   (4)   (5)

to act like my _____ . When I have a _____ , they want
(6)   (7)

to know everything about him. When he comes to the _____ , they
(8)

grill him with a hundred _____ . It is hard having five
(9)

_____ .
(10)

THE VERBS *GO, GOES, WENT,* AND *WILL GO*

Fill in each blank with **go**, **goes**, **went**, or **will go**.

1. My fiancé _____ for his blood tests yesterday.

2. I _____ to have my blood drawn tomorrow.

3. We _____ to the courthouse for our license earlier.

4. James _____ to a small church.

5. I _____ to a much larger church.

GO ON TO THE NEXT PAGE

DESCRIBING WORDS (ADVERBS)

Fill in each blank with an adverb from the following list. Use each adverb **only once**.

ADVERB LIST

down   inside   nearby   suddenly   tomorrow

1. I will see you _____ .

2. The car accident happened _____ .

3. Put that _____ on the ground.

4. Carry those _____ out of the rain.

5. The storm came on _____ .

THE WORDS *A* AND *AN*

Put **a** or **an** before each of the following.

1. ____ undergarment

2. ____ homemaker

3. ____ happy worker

4. ____ island

5. ____ history test

6. ____ tired person

7. ____ unusual person

8. ____ silly idea

9. ____ early date

10. ____ animal lover

WRITING ADDRESSES

Write each of the following sentences over. Add necessary commas.

1. Artie and I are moving to Akron Ohio.

_____

2. The twins are building a house in Nashville Tennessee.

_____

3. My parents live in Brooklyn New York.

_____

GO ON TO THE NEXT PAGE

4. My company is moving to Atlanta Georgia.

_____

5. I recently moved here from Detroit Michigan.

_____

WRITING THE TIME OF DAY

Write the following times correctly.

1. 410 am   _____   **4.** 1245 pm   _____

2. 1000 pm   _____   **5.** 715 am   _____

3. 305 am   _____

SPELLING

Add the **ed** ending to each of the following words. Double the final consonant if necessary.

1. fan _____   **5.** jump _____   **8.** cry _____

2. pet _____   **6.** dress _____   **9.** top _____

3. work _____   **7.** ban _____   **10.** pat _____

4. spot _____

ALPHABETIZING

Here are forty words. Write them in alphabetical order. Put commas between the words.

fade	happy	an	fail	face	hand	fake	ant	fall	answer
ham	crow	fame	bad	bone	fat	crime	had	favor	bag
case	hall	far	bail	call	creep	fast	boss	came	bow
cave	fan	boil	both	care	cat	cab	box	cape	crawl

_____

_____

_____

_____

_____

STOP CHECK YOUR ANSWERS BEGINNING ON PAGE 143.

Count how many items you answered correctly in each **Section** of the Chapter Three Review. Write your score per section in the **My Scores** column. If all of your section scores are as high as the **Good Scores**, go on to Chapter Four. If any of your section scores are lower than the **Good Scores**, study the lessons on the assigned **Review Pages** again before you go on to Chapter Four.

Section	Good Scores	My Scores	Review Pages
Capitalizing (Names of Countries)	4 or 5		44–45
Sentence Parts	4 or 5		46
Shortening Sentences with Commas	4 or 5		47–48
Word Order in Sentences and Commas	4 or 5		49
Naming Words (Nouns)	8, 9, or 10		50
The Verbs **Go**, **Goes**, **Went**, and **Will Go**	4 or 5		51–52
Describing Words (Adverbs)	4 or 5		53
The Words **A** and **An**	8, 9, or 10		54
Writing Addresses	4 or 5		55–56
Writing the Time of Day	4 or 5		57
Spelling	8, 9, or 10		58
Alphabetizing	All Correct		59

CAPITALIZING

Try it out.

Write the following sentences over. Capitalize correctly.

1. mr. and mrs. alvin j. warren were both born in may.

   _____

   _____

2. karen a. garcia and i are meeting on monday.

   _____

   _____

3. the boswells and the murphys are coming here in march.

   _____

   _____

4. ken l. sato and susan hall are getting married on tuesday.

   _____

   _____

5. frank valdo and chris kelly are going hunting in december.

   _____

   _____

STOP CHECK ANSWERS ON PAGE 144.

WRITING SENTENCES

Read the following:

Here are some complete subjects and verbs.

COMPLETE SUBJECTS	VERBS
Jeff and Barbara	run, play
The children and their mother	read, write
The basketball player and his buddy	drink, eat

Now read the following:

Here are the subjects and verbs in sentences.

Jeff and Barbara run and play tennis on Mondays.

The children and their mother read and write together.

The basketball player and his buddy drink and eat too much.

Did you notice?

Each complete subject contains two nouns.

There are two verbs in each predicate.

Try it out.

Write five sentences. Use the complete subject and the two verbs provided for each sentence.

1. COMPLETE SUBJECT: My boss and his wife

   VERBS: jog, swim

   _____

2. COMPLETE SUBJECT: The students and their dates

   VERBS: dance, sing

   _____

3. COMPLETE SUBJECT: The salesmen and their bosses

   VERBS: talk, joke

   _____

GO ON TO THE NEXT PAGE

4. COMPLETE SUBJECT: The homeless man and woman

VERBS: eat, sleep

_____

5. COMPLETE SUBJECT: The fire fighters and police

VERBS: save, help

_____

STOP CHECK SAMPLE ANSWERS ON PAGE 144.

COMBINING SENTENCES

Read the following:

These three sentences have the same subject but different verbs.

José jogs well.

José swims well.

José plays basketball well.

Now read the following:

This sentence combines those three sentences.

José jogs, swims, and plays basketball well.

Did you notice?

In the combined sentence, there are commas between the verbs.
The word **and** goes before the last verb.
The word **well** is used only once in the combined sentence.
Well describes all three verbs: **jogs**, **swims**, and **plays**.

Try it out.

Write one sentence that combines each set of three sentences.

1. Mallory studies piano. Mallory practices piano. Mallory teaches piano.

   _____

2. Flores cooks well. Flores bakes well. Flores irons well.

   _____

3. Barry works every day. Barry exercises every day. Barry eats every day.

   _____

4. Emily teaches at school. Emily plays the piano. Emily goes horseback riding.

   _____

5. The rain cleans the earth. The rain waters the plants. The rain fills the lakes.

   _____

STOP   CHECK ANSWERS ON PAGE 144.

SHORTENING SENTENCES WITH COMMAS

Read the following:

The children ran and played and screamed too much.
The children ran, played, and screamed too much.

Did you notice?

The sentence has three verbs.
Commas (,) help to shorten sentences that have three or more verbs.
They replace **and**—except for the last **and**—in a list of verbs.

Try it out.

Rewrite the following sentences. Shorten them by using commas.

1. The strikers carried signs and marched and yelled.

_____

_____

2. They sang songs and drank coffee and ate doughnuts.

_____

_____

3. The bosses ran the machines and answered the phones and filled the orders.

_____

_____

4. The union leaders talked to the strikers and met with the bosses and walked the picket line.

_____

_____

5. Passersby waved and talked and smiled at the strikers.

_____

_____

STOP CHECK ANSWERS ON PAGE 145.

SHORTENING SENTENCES WITH COMMAS

Read the following:

Patrick drinks a lot and eats a lot and sleeps a lot.
Patrick drinks, eats, and sleeps a lot.

I shopped earlier and met friends earlier and ate out earlier.
I shopped, met friends, and ate out earlier.

Did you notice?

The words **a lot** are used only once in the first shortened sentence.
The word **earlier** is used only once in the second shortened sentence.

Do you remember?

Commas replace **and**—except for the last **and**—in a list.

Try it out.

Rewrite the following sentences. Shorten them by using commas.

1. Henri and Eleanor work together and play together and go to school
   together.

   _____

   _____

2. Carlos read a book last night and listened to music last night and
   talked to a friend last night.

   _____

   _____

3. We are taking canoeing next term and learning to swim next term and
   joining a club next term.

   _____

   _____

GO ON TO THE NEXT PAGE

4. The mechanics located the problem and diagnosed the problem and fixed the problem.

_____

_____

5. We eat cereal in the morning and drink orange juice in the morning and read the paper in the morning.

_____

_____

STOP CHECK ANSWERS ON PAGE 145.

DESCRIBING WORDS (ADVERBS)

Read the following:

The angry man shouted at me.
The man shouted angrily at me.

Did you notice?

The word **angry**, in the first sentence, describes **man**, a noun.
The word **angrily**, in the second sentence, describes **shouted**, a verb.
Angry, an adjective, becomes **angrily**, an adverb, by the addition of the **ly** ending.
When the **ly** ending is added to a word that ends with **y**, the **y** is changed to **i**.

Try it out.

Change the following adjectives to adverbs by adding an **ly** ending.

1. happy _____

2. crazy _____

3. sad _____

4. noisy _____

5. easy _____

6. steady _____

7. strong _____

8. high _____

9. nice _____

10. kind _____

STOP CHECK ANSWERS ON PAGE 145.

THE PRONOUNS *HIM* AND *HER*

Read the following:

Give the letter to her.
The letter is about him.
There is a bug on him.
I have nothing against her.
Who is behind him?
That is nice of her to do that.
I will go with him.
Who works under her?

Did you notice?

The pronouns **her** and **him** are used after words like **to, about, on, against, under, behind, of,** and **with**.

Try it out.

Fill in each blank with the correct word.

1. Sarah's boyfriend put his arm around _____. (**she** or **her**)

2. Then he put his coat on _____. (**she** or **her**)

3. Sarah and _____ are getting married soon. (**he** or **him**)

4. _____ are not having a large wedding. (**She, He,** or **They**)

5. Everyone is very happy for _____. (**they, she, he,** or **him**)

6. _____ is a nice man. (**She, He, Her, Him,** or **They**)

7. We do not know much about _____. (**she** or **her**)

8. Her parents and _____ moved here a few months ago.
   (**she** or **her**)

9. Sarah was introduced to _____ at a party. (**he** or **him**)

10. He fell in love with _____ immediately. (**she** or **her**)

STOP   CHECK ANSWERS ON PAGE 145.

76

SHORTENING WORDS (CONTRACTIONS)

Read the following:

I have	I've
you have	you've
he has	he's
she has	she's
it has	it's
we have	we've
they have	they've

Did you notice?

The pronouns **I**, **you**, **he**, **she**, **it**, **we**, and **they** can be joined by **has** or **have**.

When a pronoun joins with **has** or **have**, the **ha** in **has** or **have** is omitted.

This mark (') replaces the omitted letters.

But notice this:

he is	he's	he has	he's
she is	she's	she has	she's
it is	it's	it has	it's

The shortened forms for **he is**, **she is**, and **it is** are the same as for **he has**, **she has**, and **it has**.

You can tell what the shortened form means only from the meaning of the sentence. For example:

It's cold today. = It is cold today.

It's been a cold day. = It has been a cold day.

Try it out.

Draw a line under each contraction. Then write the two words that make up each contraction.

1. They've had a week to think about it. _____

2. I'm not going. _____

3. She's done a lot for you. _____

4. We can say we're going. _____

GO ON TO THE NEXT PAGE

5. Gloria says they're very rich. _____

6. I've more important things to do. _____

7. It's too bad about that. _____

8. She's really very nice. _____

9. He's spent a lot of money on the party. _____

10. She's going to be angry. _____

STOP CHECK ANSWERS ON PAGE 145.

USING *YES* AND *NO* IN A SENTENCE

Read the following:

Yes, that is a good idea.
No, I am not going to the party.
Yes, Jim is at work.
No, Sue is not staying home tonight.

Did you notice?

A comma (,) follows **Yes** or **No** at the beginning of a sentence.

Try it out.

Write the following sentences over. Capitalize and add commas and end marks correctly.

1. yes help is on the way

   _____

2. yes i am happily married

   _____

3. no she does not want to go

   _____

4. no mary did not say something else

   _____

5. yes the room is very messy

   _____

6. no i do not like that dress

   _____

GO ON TO THE NEXT PAGE

7. yes everyone i know will be there

_____

8. yes i agree with you

_____

9. no it is not too much

_____

10. yes it is too much for me

_____

STOP CHECK ANSWERS ON PAGE 145.

WRITING DATES

Read the following:

John will graduate from high school on <u>June 9, 1990</u>.
I was married on <u>May 7, 1960</u>.
My husband was born on <u>January 1, 1939</u>.

Did you notice?

Each sentence has a date in it.
The date is made up of the month, the day, and the year.
There is a comma (,) between the day and the year.

Try it out.

Write the following sentences over. Capitalize and add commas and end marks correctly.

1. beatrice moved to texas on may 2 1986

_____

2. mike arrived in new york on july 17 1987

_____

3. hiro and kimiko were married in denver on april 13 1978

_____

4. michelle went to philadelphia on january 20 1988

_____

5. kathy will move to cleveland on september 14 1989

_____

STOP CHECK ANSWERS ON PAGE 145.

WRITING AN INVITATION

Read the following:

December 21, 1989

Dear Maria,

   I'm having a New Year's Eve party at my home on
Saturday, December 31, starting at 9:00 P.M. Please,
phone to let me know if you can come. My phone number is
555-3254.

   I hope you can come to my party. I'm looking forward to
seeing you.

Yours truly,

Georgette

Did you notice?

In the date, a comma separates the day from the year.
Both words in the greeting, **Dear Maria**, begin with capital letters.
There is a comma after the greeting.
The first word of every paragraph is indented.
The left edge of the body of the letter is in line with the greeting.
In the closing, the first word, **Yours**, begins with a capital letter.
There is a comma after the closing.

Did you know?

An invitation tells the day, date, time, place of, and reason for a party.

GO ON TO THE NEXT PAGE

Try it out.

Write an invitation to ask someone to a birthday party you are giving for a friend at your house.

STOP CHECK THE SAMPLE LETTER ON PAGE 145.

WRITING AN INVITATION

Read the following:

February 3, 1990

Dear Dave,

   I would like to invite you to a dinner party at my home
on Saturday, February 12, at 7:30 P.M. Please, phone to
let me know if you can come. My phone number is 555-6498.

               Your friend,

               Daniella

Do you remember?

In a letter, commas are used in the date and after the greeting and the closing.

Both words in the greeting and the first word in the closing are capitalized.

Paragraphs are indented, but the left edge of the body is in line with the greeting.

An invitation gives the day, date, time, place of, and reason for a party.

GO ON TO THE NEXT PAGE

Try it out.

Write a letter inviting someone to a party at your house.

SPELLING

Read the following:

| get | getting | hit | hitting |
| beg | begging | run | running |

Did you notice?

Each of these words has one vowel: **get**, **beg**, **hit**, **run**.
One consonant follows the vowel in each word.
When an **ing** ending is added to such a word, the final consonant is doubled.

Now read the following:

In each of the following words, there are two vowels together or two final consonants.
No change is made when the **ing** ending is added.

| boil | boiling | mail | mailing |
| cook | cooking | calm | calming |

Try it out.

Add the **ing** ending to each of the following words. Double the final consonant if necessary.

1. can _____
2. fit _____
3. chat _____
4. sail _____
5. trim _____
6. fan _____
7. wrap _____
8. fail _____
9. trail _____
10. chop _____

11. load _____
12. sun _____
13. let _____
14. look _____
15. stop _____
16. grab _____
17. trap _____
18. dial _____
19. keep _____
20. meet _____

STOP CHECK ANSWERS ON PAGE 146.

ALPHABETIZING

Try it out.

Here are lists of people's names. Write each list in alphabetical order. Put commas between the names in the lists you write.

1. Fred Gable   Martin Gomez   Anthony Green   Seth Guzman

   James Garcia   Jean Gerber   Hank Gonzalez   Betty Grable

   _____

   _____

   _____

2. John Powers   Don Payton   Fred Pain   Sally Pear

   Joan Pace   Richad Patton Francis Parrot Ann Pane

   _____

   _____

   _____

3. Charles Donne   Edward Dean   Gloria Davis   Marcie Daniels

   Donna Dempsy   James Bear   Fred Drake   Susan Dale

   _____

   _____

   _____

GO ON TO THE NEXT PAGE

4. Frank Sallo   Frank Sartino   Geroge Samley   Lawrence Saab

    Maria Satos   Carol Sable   José Sanchez   Kenneth Sachs

_____

_____

5. Walter Brunn   Robert Breck   Donald Brine   Kathleen Brown

    Alice Bennett   Cynthia Baker   Daniel Braun   Angela Booker

_____

_____

STOP CHECK ANSWERS ON PAGE 146.

CAPITALIZING

Write the following sentences over. Capitalize correctly.

1. my fiancé and i can't afford a big wedding.

   _____

2. we are getting married in june and moving to california.

   _____

3. our parents live in maine and are upset about our moving to california.

   _____

4. my parents' friends, mr. and mrs. s. shibata, helped us a lot.

   _____

5. march, april, and may will be very busy months for betty and me.

   _____

WRITING SENTENCES

Write five sentences. Use the complete subject and the two verbs provided for each sentence.

1. COMPLETE SUBJECT: George and I

   VERBS: returned, relaxed

   _____

2. COMPLETE SUBJECT: The old man and his wife

   VERBS: enjoy, do

   _____

3. COMPLETE SUBJECT: My girlfriend and her sister

   VERBS: dance, sing

   _____

GO ON TO THE NEXT PAGE

4. COMPLETE SUBJECT: The hungry child and her brother

VERBS: cried, asked

_____

5. COMPLETE SUBJECT: Greg and his family

VERBS: argue, fight

_____

COMBINING SENTENCES

Write one sentence that combines each set of three sentences.

1. The twins work together.
   The twins play together.
   The twins stay together.

   _____

2. That man looks very strange.
   That man acts very strange.
   The man seems very strange.

   _____

3. The homeless man screamed.
   The homeless man jumped.
   The homeless man cursed at people.

   _____

4. The lost child ate some food.
   The lost child drank some soda.
   The lost child played with the police officer.

   _____

5. The child's mother searched for her child.
   The child's mother cried.
   The child's mother went to the police.

   _____

GO ON TO THE NEXT PAGE

SHORTENING SENTENCES WITH COMMAS

Write the following sentences over. Shorten them by using commas.

1. The city can be an exciting place and a great place and a fun place to live.

   _____

2. The city can also be an unfriendly place and a dangerous place and a frightening place to live.

   _____

3. Dan drinks too much and smokes too much and works too much.

   _____

4. My job tires me a lot and bores me a lot and depresses me a lot.

   _____

5. I want to get married and raise a family and have a nice house.

   _____

DESCRIBING WORDS (ADVERBS)

Change the following adjectives into adverbs by adding an **ly** ending.

1. sad _____
2. slow _____
3. careful _____
4. proud _____
5. glad _____

6. swift _____
7. quick _____
8. short _____
9. happy _____
10. angry _____

THE PRONOUNS *HIM* AND *HER*

Fill in each blank with the correct word.

1. This letter is for _____. (**he** or **him**)

2. It is wrong of _____ to do that. (**she** or **her**)

3. I did not speak badly about _____. (**she** or **her**)

4. That coat looks nice on _____. (**him** or **he**)

5. Is that for _____? (**him** or **he**)

GO ON TO THE NEXT PAGE

SHORTENING WORDS (CONTRACTIONS)

Write the word or words that make up each contraction.

1. can't _____   6. I'll _____

2. hasn't _____   7. she's _____

3. haven't _____   8. I've _____

4. they've _____   9. she'll _____

5. it's _____   10. they're _____

USING YES AND NO IN A SENTENCE

Write the following sentences over. Capitalize and add commas and end marks correctly.

1. no i can't stay

_____

2. yes benita will be here soon

_____

3. yes that is very nice

_____

4. no she is not being fair

_____

5. yes i will marry bill

_____

WRITING DATES

Write the following dates over. Capitalize and add commas correctly.

1. may 4 1990 _____

2. february 11 1932 _____

3. november 3 1927 _____

4. august 9 1941 _____

5. january 1 1988 _____

GO ON TO THE NEXT PAGE

WRITING AN INVITATION

Write an invitation to ask someone to a birthday party.

_____

_____

_____

_____

_____

_____

_____

_____

SPELLING

Add the **ing** ending to each of the following words. Double the final consonant if necessary.

1. run   _____   6. play   _____

2. pet   _____   7. get   _____

3. hit   _____   8. set   _____

4. wrap   _____   9. trap   _____

5. spot   _____   10. plan   _____

GO ON TO THE NEXT PAGE

ALPHABETIZING

Write these twenty names in alphabetical order. Put commas between the names in your list.

Mary Meklo   Alice Addison   Richard Drake   David Meger

Alvin Mein   Frank Means   Dorothy Mecker   Jack Adler

José Mondez   Joseph Melm   Donald Dreyer   George Mebber

Alan Meeker   Sara Ment   Sam Memer   Dale Ackers

Frank May   Susan Cramer   Sally Abrams   Sally Dugan

_____

_____

_____

_____

_____

STOP   CHECK YOUR ANSWERS BEGINNING ON PAGE 146.

Count how many items you answered correctly in each **Section** of the Chapter Four Review. Write your score per section in the **My Scores** column. If all of your section scores are as high as the **Good Scores**, go on to Chapter Five. If any of your section scores are lower than the **Good Scores**, study the lessons on the assigned **Review Pages** again before you go on to Chapter Five.

Section	Good Scores	My Scores	Review Pages
Capitalizing	4 or 5		68
Writing Sentences	4 or 5		69–70
Combining Sentences	4 or 5		71
Shortening Sentences with Commas	4 or 5		72–74
Describing Words (Adverbs)	8, 9, or 10		75
The Pronouns **Him** and **Her**	4 or 5		76
Shortening Words (Contractions)	8, 9, or 10		77–78
Using **Yes** and **No** in a Sentence	4 or 5		79–80
Writing Dates	4 or 5		81
Writing an Invitation	A correct invitation		82–85
Spelling	8, 9, or 10		86
Alphabetizing	All correct		87–88

CAPITALIZING

Try it out.

Write the following sentences over. Capitalize correctly.

1. my sister and i share an apartment on river avenue in boston.

_____

_____

2. she and i moved here from detroit last august.

_____

_____

3. our divorced parents moved from france to the united states.

_____

_____

4. our mother, mrs. audrey adams, remarried and lives in new jersey.

_____

_____

5. our father, mr. anthony brandt, lives in washington, d.c.

_____

_____

STOP   CHECK ANSWERS ON PAGE 147.

COMBINING SENTENCES

Read the following:

Beng Choo is pretty.
Marie is pretty.
Flores is pretty.

Now read the following:

This sentence combines those three sentences:

Beng Choo, Marie, and Flores are pretty.

Did you notice?

In the combined sentence there are commas between the nouns in the complete subject.
The word **and** goes before the last noun.
The combined sentence describes more than one person, so **are** replaces **is**.

Try it out.

Write one sentence that combines each set of three sentences.

1. Sally loves to dance.
   Mark loves to dance.
   Pedro loves to dance.

   _____

2. Mr. McCall lives on Main Street.
   Miss Otis lives on Main Street.
   Ms. Franco lives on Main Street.

   _____

3. My mother is nice.
   My father is nice.
   My sister is nice.

   _____

GO ON TO THE NEXT PAGE

4. This pig lives on a farm.
This cow lives on a farm.
This goat lives on a farm.

_____

5. Mrs. Meltzer is happy.
Valerie is happy.
Ali is happy

_____

STOP CHECK ANSWERS ON PAGE 147.

SHORTENING SENTENCES WITH COMMAS

Read the following:

The girl is pretty and cheerful and nice.
The girl is pretty, cheerful, and nice.

I fell sad and depressed and gloomy.
I feel sad, depressed, and gloomy.

Did you notice?

Each sentence has three adjectives after the verb.
Commas help to shorten sentences with several adjectives after the verb.
They replace **and**—except for the last **and**—in a list of adjectives.

But notice this:

When there are only two adjectives after the verb, no commas are used.

Carl is friendly and nice.
Donna seems slim and trim.

Try it out.

Some of the following sentences can be shortened by using commas. Rewrite those that can be shortened.

1. The bus is hot and crowded.

   _____

2. At night the city looks dark and lonely and frightening.

   _____

3. My boyfriend is a charming and handsome and clever man.

   _____

4. He always feels cheerful and hopeful.

   _____

5. I seem dull and crabby and ugly next to him.

   _____

STOP CHECK ANSWERS ON PAGE 147.

SHORTENING SENTENCES WITH COMMAS

Read the following:

Teresa and José are friendly and cheerful and nice.
Teresa and José are friendly, cheerful, and nice.

The house is dirty and unpainted and falling apart.
The house is dirty, unpainted, and falling apart.

The students are noisy and excited.

The trucker is tired and sleepy.

Do you remember?

Commas help to shorten sentences that have three or more adjectives after the verb.
They replace **and**—except for the last **and**—in a list of adjectives.
No comma is needed when only two adjectives follow the verb.

Try it out.

Write the following sentences over. Shorten them by using commas.

1. The snow was white and clean and deep.

   _____

2. The robber was masked and tall and fat.

   _____

3. The robber's dog was filthy and stinking and dangerous.

   _____

4. The police were brave and strong and caring.

   _____

5. The victims were frightened and upset and tired.

   _____

STOP CHECK ANSWERS ON PAGE 148.

DESCRIBING WORDS AND LINKING WORDS

Read the following:
The adjectives are underlined in these sentences.

The <u>chocolate</u> cake tastes <u>good</u>.

You look <u>beautiful</u>.

Eleni seems <u>sad</u>.

Artie feels <u>happy</u>.

The <u>man-made</u> lakes are <u>dirty</u>.

The <u>man-made</u> lake smells <u>unclean</u>.

Did you notice?
The words **chocolate**, **good**, **beautiful**, **sad**, **happy**, **man-made**, **dirty**, and **unclean** are describing words, or **adjectives**.
They tell something about the subject of the sentence.
Describing words that tell about the subject can come before the subject.
They can also come after verbs, such as **taste**, **look**, **seem**, **feel**, **smell**, and **are**.

Do you remember?
The simple subject of a sentence is a noun or a pronoun.
Adjectives describe nouns or pronouns.

Try it out.
Draw a line under each of the describing words in these sentences.

1. The young groom looked worried and afraid.

2. His unlined face appeared pale and tight.

3. His pretty bride looked calm and joyful.

4. The proud parents looked tense and confused.

5. The jolly minister looked pleased and happy.

GO ON TO THE NEXT PAGE

6. The guests seemed impatient and uneasy.

7. The children yawned and looked tired and unhappy.

8. The lovely flowers still looked beautiful.

9. The large church seemed empty.

10. Everyone was happy to see the couple kiss.

STOP CHECK ANSWERS ON PAGE 148.

DESCRIBING WORDS (ADVERBS)

Read the following:

The cheerful man greeted me.
The man greeted me cheerfully.

Did you notice?

In the first sentence the word **cheerful** describes **man**, a noun.
In the second sentence the word **cheerfully** describes **greeted**, the verb.
The adjective becomes an adverb by adding the letters **ly**.

Try it out.

Change the following adjectives into adverbs.

1. proud _____

2. careful _____

3. quiet _____

4. clear _____

5. beautiful _____

6. cheerful _____

7. swift _____

8. rude _____

9. careless _____

10. loud _____

STOP CHECK ANSWERS ON PAGE 148.

DESCRIBING WORDS (ADJECTIVES AND ADVERBS)

Read the following:

The describing words are underlined in these sentences.

The <u>old</u> man moved <u>slowly</u>.

A <u>new</u> store opened <u>yesterday</u>.

Did you notice?

The words **old** and **new** describe the simple subjects, **man** and **store**. They are adjectives.

The words **slowly** and **yesterday** describe the verbs, **moved** and **opened**.

They are adverbs.

Try it out.

Choose two words to add to each of the following sentences. Write an adjective in the first blank and an adverb in the second blank.

1. The _____ lady ate _____.

   (slowly, dumbly, beautiful)

2. The _____ plane landed _____.

   (tired, safely, small)

3. My _____ friend arrived _____.

   (tomorrow, good, yesterday)

4. My _____ girlfriend speaks _____.

   (smartly, smart, softly)

5. His _____ boss will work _____.

   (before, tomorrow, tired)

6. The _____ dog barked _____.

   (weakly, tomorrow, old)

GO ON TO THE NEXT PAGE

7. The _____ person screamed _____.

(**shortly, loudly, frightened**)

8. My _____ boyfriend dances _____.

(**nicely, lately, handsome**)

9. The _____ animal drinks _____.

(**quickly, brightly, small**)

10. A _____ pilot flies _____.

(**heavily, carefully, good**)

STOP CHECK ANSWERS ON PAGE 148.

THE PRONOUN *THEM*

Read the following:

Matthew gave the job to them.
Veldez spoke well of them.
Sue put a name tag on them.
I do not know anything about them.
What is on the floor under them?
What do you have against them?
What is behind them?
She is with them.

Did you notice?

The pronoun **them** is used after such words as **to**, **of**, **on**, **about**, **under**, **against**, **behind**, and **with**.

Try it out.

Fill in each blank with **they** or **them**.

1. No one is speaking to _____.

2. _____ both tell lots of lies.

3. Claude refuses to work with _____.

4. We think about _____ all the time.

5. Did _____ tell you that?

6. What do you have against _____?

7. Is that snow on _____?

8. What is under _____?

9. _____ refused to go.

10. Did we give it to _____?

STOP   CHECK ANSWERS ON PAGE 148.

WRITING THE TIME OF DAY

Read the following:

Twenty-five minutes after nine in the morning is 9:25 A.M.
Thirty-five minutes after eleven at night is 11:35 P.M.
Seven o'clock in the evening is 7:00 P.M.

Do you remember?

A.M. and **P.M.** are written with capital letters and periods.
There is a colon (:) between the hour and the minutes in the time.

Did you know?

A.M. is the time after midnight and before noon.
P.M. is the time after noon and before midnight.

Try it out.

Write each time with **A.M.** or **P.M.**

1. Half-past eight in the morning is ———————— .

2. Twenty minutes past four in the afternoon is ———————— .

3. Six o'clock in the evening is ———————— .

4. Half-past eleven in the morning is ———————— .

5. Fifteen minutes after six in the morning is ———————— .

6. Eleven o'clock at night is ———————— .

7. Four o'clock in the morning is ———————— .

8. Ten minutes past three in the morning is ———————— .

9. Five minutes past five in the evening is ———————— .

10. Forty-five minutes past one in the afternoon is ———————— .

STOP CHECK ANSWERS ON PAGE 148.

WRITING THE TIME OF DAY

Read the following:

Do you really have to get to work at 8:00 P.M.?
I get up a 7:30 A.M. during the week.
On Sundays I get up at 9:00 A.M.

Did you notice?

When **A.M.** or **P.M.** comes at the end of a statement, there is no extra period.
When **A.M.** or **P.M.** comes at the end of a question, there is also a question mark.

Do you remember?

A.M. and **P.M.** are written with capital letters and periods.
There is a colon (:) between the hour and the minutes in the time.

Try it out.

Write the following sentences over. Capitalize and add colons, periods, and end marks correctly.

1. i am getting up at 830 am tomorrow

   _____

2. do you want me to awaken you at 645 am

   _____

3. will you be able to leave work at 550 pm

   _____

4. is it 1100 pm already

   _____

5. patty and kim are arriving at 1045 am

   _____

STOP CHECK ANSWERS ON PAGE 148.

WRITING A FRIENDLY LETTER

Read the following:

> January 2, 1990
>
> Dear Marie,
>
>   Happy New Year! I just wanted to write a short note to tell you that I enjoyed your dinner party yesterday. The food was excellent, and you were a wonderful hostess.
>
>   Love,
>
>   Hiro

Do you remember?

In a date, a comma separates the day from the year.
Both words in a greeting, like **Dear Marie**, begin with capital letters.
There is a comma after a greeting.
The first word of a paragraph is indented.
The left edge of the body of a letter is in line with the greeting.
The first word or the only word of a closing, like **Love**, begins with a capital letter.
There is a comma after a closing.

GO ON TO THE NEXT PAGE

Try it out.

Write a friendly letter to thank someone whose party you attended.

STOP CHECK SAMPLE LETTER ON PAGE 148.

ADDRESSING AN ENVELOPE

Read the following:

```
Jennifer A. Rizzoli
719 Stuart Road              ←———— sender
Columbus, Ohio 43017



           person receiving    Mrs. Sharon Gates
               letter ———→     910 East Main Street
                               Monticello, Arkansas 71602
```

Did you notice?

The sender's address goes in the top left corner of the envelope.
The address of the person receiving the letter goes in the center of the
envelope.

Try it out.

Here is an envelope. Address it to a friend. You are the sender of the letter.

```
_____


_____


_____



                      _____


                      _____


                      _____
```

STOP CHECK SAMPLE ENVELOPE ON PAGE 148.

SPELLING

Try it out.

Add the **ing** ending to each word. Double the final consonant if necessary.

1. blame _____
2. come _____
3. hope _____
4. make _____
5. hop _____
6. run _____
7. fake _____
8. rake _____
9. sit _____
10. wake _____

11. boil _____
12. fan _____
13. sit _____
14. burn _____
15. stop _____
16. file _____
17. keep _____
18. take _____
19. state _____
20. fill _____

STOP CHECK ANSWERS ON PAGE 148.

ALPHABETIZING (USING THE DICTIONARY)

Did you know?

A dictionary has guide words at the top of each page.
The guide words tell which are the first and last words on the page.
All words between the two guide words are on that page in alphabetical order.

Now read the following:

Here is a sample of the guide words at the top of a dictionary page.

fine	**flat**

Did you notice?

The word **fine** is the first word on the page.
The word **flat** is the last word on the page.
The word **five** would be on this page.
The word **fail** would not be on this page. It would come before this page.

Try it out.

Use the guide words **fine** and **flat** to answer the following questions.

1. Is the word **first** on this page? _____

2. Is the word **file** on this page? _____

3. Is the word **fool** on this page? _____

4. Is the word **fist** on this page? _____

5. Is the word **fear** on this page? _____

6. Is the word **fix** on this page? _____

7. Is the word **fifth** on this page? _____

8. Is the word **fight** on this page? _____

9. Is the word **fire** on this page? _____

10. Is the word **flame** on this page? _____

STOP CHECK ANSWERS ON PAGE 149.

CAPITALIZING

Write the following sentences over. Capitalize correctly.

1. miss anne j. kelly lives on west street in detroit.

_____

2. on tuesday mr. and mrs. alvin j. cole are going to miami, florida.

_____

3. on friday ms. moon and i are driving to atlanta, georgia.

_____

4. mr. ortez and miss torres came to new york city from spain.

_____

5. eduardo, julio, ruby, and i are leaving on wednesday for italy.

_____

COMBINING SENTENCES

Write one sentence that combines each set of three sentences.

1. Gregory does well in everything.
   Mariquita does well in everything.
   Seth does well in everything.

_____

2. Yoshiko lives in California.
   Laura lives in California.
   Terry lives in California.

_____

3. David just bought clothes.
   Brad just bought clothes.
   Gloria just bought clothes.

_____

GO ON TO THE NEXT PAGE

4. Henry won the lottery.
   Margaret won the lottery.
   I won the lottery.

   _____

5. The animals look frightened.
   The men look frightened.
   The women look frightened.

   _____

SHORTENING SENTENCES WITH COMMAS

Write the following sentences over. Shorten them by using commas.

1. The play was funny and sad and different.

   _____

2. That man is handsome and tall and smart.

   _____

3. Kerry seems lonely and frightened and worried.

   _____

4. The clown looks old and sad and tired.

   _____

5. Mack is angry and annoyed and unhappy.

   _____

DESCRIBING WORDS AND LINKING WORDS

Draw a line under each of the describing words.

1. The unhappy child seems tired.

2. The old woman looks sad.

3. Flores feels angry about that.

4. The rude person looks mean.

5. The handsome man is not young.

GO ON TO THE NEXT PAGE

DESCRIBING WORDS (ADVERBS)
Change the following adjectives into adverbs.

1. correct _____
2. cruel _____
3. calm _____
4. crude _____
5. careful _____

6. fierce _____
7. mean _____
8. joyful _____
9. careless _____
10. clear _____

THE PRONOUN *THEM*
Fill in each blank with **they** or **them**.

1. I gave it to _____ earlier.

2. _____ told me not to worry.

3. I don't hold it against _____.

4. Do _____ know about _____?

5. _____ put that away some time ago.

WRITING THE TIME OF DAY
Write each time in numbers with **A.M.** or **P.M.**

1. A quarter past nine in the evening _____

2. Ten minutes past two in the morning _____

3. Half past one in the afternoon _____

4. Twenty-five minutes past eleven at night _____

5. Five minutes past four in the morning _____

GO ON TO THE NEXT PAGE

WRITING A FRIENDLY LETTER

Write a friendly letter to thank someone for having taken you out to lunch.

ADDRESSING AN ENVELOPE

Here is an envelope. Address it to the person you wrote your thank-you letter to. You are the sender of the letter.

GO ON TO THE NEXT PAGE

SPELLING

Add the **ing** ending to each word. Double the final consonant if necessary.

1. rake _____   6. time _____

2. take _____   7. wake _____

3. make _____   8. hate _____

4. greet _____   9. cry _____

5. hit _____   10. pile _____

ALPHABETIZING (USING THE DICTIONARY)

Use the guide words **caller** and **carrot** to answer these questions. Write **Yes** or **No** in each blank.

1. Is the word **came** on this page? _____

2. Is the word **cattle** on this page? _____

3. Is the word **cape** on this page? _____

4. Is the word **cage** on this page? _____

5. Is the word **castle** on this page? _____

STOP CHECK YOUR ANSWERS BEGINNING ON PAGE 149.

Count how many items you answered correctly in each **Section** of the Chapter Five Review. Write your score per section in the **My Scores** column. If all of your section scores are as high as the **Good Scores**, take the Posttest. If any of your section scores are lower than the **Good Scores**, study the lessons on the assigned **Review Pages** again before you take the Posttest.

Section	Good Scores	My Scores	Review Pages
Capitalizing	4 or 5		98
Combining Sentences	4 or 5		99–100
Shortening Sentences With Commas	4 or 5		101–102
Describing Words and Linking Words	4 or 5		103–104
Describing Words (Adverbs)	8, 9, or 10		105–107
The Pronoun **Them**	4 or 5		108
Writing the Time of Day	4 or 5		109–110
Writing a Friendly Letter	A correct letter		111–112
Addressing an Envelope	Correct addresses		113
Spelling	8, 9, or 10		114
Alphabetizing (Using the Dictionary)	4 or 5		115

CAPITALIZING

Write the following sentences over. Capitalize correctly. Remember to put quotation marks around short story and poem titles.

1. mr. and mrs. oliver m. collins live on york avenue in dallas, texas.

   _____

2. ms. anderson and her friend carla are visiting italy and spain next winter.

   _____

3. have you read "my life is an open book"?

   _____

4. the poem "i'm an only child and i love it" is very funny.

   _____

5. The silbys moved in september from washington, d.c., to omaha, nebraska.

   _____

COMPOUND SUBJECTS AND VERBS IN SENTENCES

Draw one line under each noun in the complete subject in each sentence. Draw two lines under each verb in each sentence.

1. The twins and their wives work and travel together.

2. Often their friends and wives mistake one twin for the other.

3. Herbert and Jack talk and walk the same.

4. Their nieces and nephews love and adore them.

5. Unfortunately, they live and work too far away from their nieces and nephews.

GO ON TO THE NEXT PAGE

SENTENCE PARTS

Find the words from Group Two, the predicate, that go with each complete subject from Group One. Write the letter in the blank.

GROUP ONE (COMPLETE SUBJECT)

___ **1.** Hate

___ **2.** Love

___ **3.** I

___ **4.** A gloomy person

___ **5.** Holidays

GROUP TWO (PREDICATE)

a. like cheerful people.

b. are lonely for people without friends.

c. can heal many wounds.

d. can only destroy.

e. is no fun to be with.

RECOGNIZING SENTENCES

Put a check (√) by each of the sentences.

☐ **1.** Into the park by the bench.

☐ **2.** The Bensons and the Garcias have.

☐ **3.** Rush there.

☐ **4.** Try to come early.

☐ **5.** Please stay a little longer.

COMBINING SENTENCES

Write one sentence that combines each set of three sentences.

1. The fruit looks good now.
The fruit smells good now.
The fruit tastes good now.

_____

2. Betty wears very pretty dresses.
Betty wears very pretty hats.
Betty wears very pretty sweaters.

_____

GO ON TO THE NEXT PAGE

3. My car needs new seat covers.
   My car needs new tires.
   My car needs new windows.

   _____

4. The police chased the robber.
   The police arrested the robber.
   The police handcuffed the robber.

   _____

5. The Chins walk fast.
   The Chins talk fast.
   The Chins eat fast.

   _____

SHORTENING SENTENCES WITH COMMAS

Rewrite the following sentences. Shorten them by using commas.

1. Mr. Charm gets up early every morning and Mr. Chase gets up early every morning and I get up early every morning.

   _____

2. My brother Peter exercises every day and my sister Heather exercises every day and I exercise every day.

   _____

3. Marie often swims at the YWCA and Judy often swims at the YWCA and Rebecca often swims at the YWCA.

   _____

4. My kitchen needs painting badly and my bedroom needs painting badly and my bathroom needs painting badly.

   _____

5. James wants to work overtime tomorrow and William wants to work overtime tomorrow and Robert wants to work overtime tomorrow.

   _____

GO ON TO THE NEXT PAGE

WORD ORDER IN SENTENCES AND COMMAS

Use the following groups of words to write sentences. Add necessary commas.

1. Scott overtime I Jeff working and are today.

   _____

2. Weekend Andy away this Dave Hossein and going are.

   _____

3. Juanita party and Ann I Year's giving a New are.

   _____

4. Aunts uncles visit parents we going to are my and.

   _____

5. School reading learning I writing arithmetic at am and.

   _____

COMMAND SENTENCES

Put the correct end mark at the end of each sentence.

1. Hold that door

2. Stand back

3. Please give her some room

4. What are you doing

5. She is fabulous

RECOGNIZING NAMING WORDS (NOUNS)

Draw a line under each of the nouns in the following short story.

I met my wife at school. She dropped her books, papers, pens, and pencils on the floor next to me. I stopped to help her. When I looked up, I saw this beautiful, smiling face. I fell in love with her immediately. All day I could only think about her.

GO ON TO THE NEXT PAGE

MORE THAN ONE (PLURAL)

Write the plural of each of the following nouns.

1. woman _____   6. table _____

2. tooth _____   7. mouse _____

3. man _____   8. child _____

4. house _____   9. lady _____

5. goose _____   10. class _____

THE PRONOUNS *I, YOU, HE, SHE, IT, WE,* AND *THEY*

Fill in each blank with **I**, **you**, **she**, **he**, **it**, **we**, or **they**

1. The world looks great to me today.

   _____ didn't look so great yesterday.

2. My father and I had a big fight.

   _____ yelled a lot at each other.

3. He told me I had to change my ways.

   _____ was very angry with him.

4. My father cares a lot for me.

   _____ wants me to do well in school.

5. My parents both have made a good home for me.

   _____ are very nice people.

THE PRONOUNS *HIM* AND *HER*

Fill in each blank with the correct word.

1. Do you feel sorry for _____? (**he** or **him**)

2. Don't talk about _____ in that way. (**she** or **her**)

3. What do you have against _____? (**she** or **her**)

4. _____ insulted my friends. (**Her** or **She**)

5. I am sending this letter to _____. (**he** or **him**)

GO ON TO THE NEXT PAGE

THE PRONOUN *THEM*

Fill in each blank with **they** or **them**.

1. Please give these things to _____.

2. I have something else for _____.

3. Are _____ here yet?

4. _____ were here a minute ago.

5. The story in the papers is about _____.

DESCRIBING WORDS AND LINKING WORDS

Draw a line under each of the describing words in these sentences.

1. The lovely young woman is charming.

2. My pretty sister is a kind person.

3. These beautiful flowers are fresh.

4. Her tiny shoes are pointed.

5. The three women in the movie are mean and ugly.

DESCRIBING WORDS (ADJECTIVES)

In the blank in each sentence, write the describing word with an **er** or **est** ending.

1. No, she is _____ than Dan. (**big**)

2. My dog is the _____ dog I have ever seen. (**fat**)

3. She is _____ than I am. (**pretty**)

4. This is the _____ present I have ever received. (**nice**)

5. Julio is the _____ person I know. (**fine**)

ACTION WORDS (VERBS)

In the blanks, write the past and future forms of each verb.

	PAST TIME	FUTURE TIME
1. play	_____	_____
2. clean	_____	_____

GO ON TO THE NEXT PAGE

	PAST TIME	FUTURE TIME
3. look	_____	_____
4. rush	_____	_____
5. turn	_____	_____

THE VERBS *GO, GOES, WENT,* AND *WILL GO*

Fill in each blank with the correct word.

1. They _____ away hours ago. (**go, goes, went, will go**)

2. Allan and Laurie _____ to Mexico soon. (**go, goes, will go**)

3. We _____ there before. (**go, goes, went, will go**)

4. I _____ home with Artie tomorrow. (**go, goes, will go**)

5. She _____ to school now. (**go, goes, went**)

THE VERBS *HAS, HAVE, HAD,* AND *WILL HAVE*

Fill in each blank with the correct word.

1. He _____ a used truck now. (**has, have**)

2. He _____ lots of problems before. (**has, have, had**)

3. We _____ a fire in it yesterday. (**has, have, had**)

4. John _____ no money to fix it now. (**has, have**)

5. I _____ no ride to work tomorrow. (**has, had, will have**)

THE VERBS *DO, DOES, DID,* AND *WILL DO*

Fill in each blank with the correct word.

1. She _____ that tomorrow. (**do, did, will do**)

2. It _____ a few things on its own before. (**do, does, did, will do**)

3. Kenji and Sachiko _____ things together now. (**do, does**)

4. We _____ nothing last week. (**do, does, did, will do**)

5. My boss _____ well now. (**do, does**)

GO ON TO THE NEXT PAGE

THE VERBS *SEE, SEES, SAW,* AND *WILL SEE*
Fill in each blank with the correct word.

1. I _____ my parents shortly. (**sees, will see, saw**)

2. My parents _____ me two months ago. (**see, sees, saw**)

3. They _____ my sisters more than me. (**see, sees**)

4. We _____ a ball game next week. (**see, saw, will see**)

5. We _____ each other only at holidays now. (**see, sees**)

RECOGNIZING DESCRIBING WORDS (ADVERBS)
Draw a line under each adverb.

1. A big black bear escaped from the zoo yesterday.

2. It roamed the streets freely.

3. The brave police searched the streets everywhere.

4. They looked for the bear yesterday and today.

5. The tired police found the bear sleeping peacefully at the zoo.

DESCRIBING WORDS (ADVERBS)
Change the following adjectives into adverbs by adding an **ly** ending.
Double the final consonant if necessary.

1. careless _____
2. fierce _____
3. short _____
4. bright _____
5. clever _____

6. fine _____
7. hopeful _____
8. nice _____
9. stupid _____
10. mean _____

WRITING THE TIME OF DAY
Write each time in numbers with **A.M.** or **P.M.**

1. A quarter past one in the morning _____

2. Twenty past three in the afternoon _____

3. Forty-five past nine at night _____

GO ON TO THE NEXT PAGE

4. Half-past seven at night   _____

5. Ten past eleven in the morning   _____

WRITING DATES
Write the following dates correctly.

1. june 25 1988   _____   **4.** november 10 1989   _____

2. october 3 1983   _____   **5.** july 4 1942   _____

3. april 8 1917   _____

WRITING ADDRESSES
Write each of the following addresses correctly.

1. 874 perry street

    atlanta georgia 30351

2. 34 second avenue

    santa fe new mexico 87505

SHORTENING WORDS (CONTRACTIONS)
Write each pair of words over as a contraction.

1. I will   _____   **6.** do not   _____

2. has not   _____   **7.** he is   _____

3. she will   _____   **8.** I have   _____

4. they are   _____   **9.** we will   _____

5. could not   _____   **10.** does not   _____

THE WORDS *A* AND *AN*
Put **a** or **an** before each of the following words.

1. _____ huge house   **6.** _____ high fence

2. _____ union card   **7.** _____ hot plate

3. _____ hourly job   **8.** _____ underwater watch

4. _____ young person   **9.** _____ ear

5. _____ ulcer   **10.** _____ unused ticket

GO ON TO THE NEXT PAGE

USING *YES* AND *NO* IN A SENTENCE
Write the following sentences over. Capitalize correctly and add necessary commas.

1. no sally and i are not friends.

   _____

2. yes she lies a lot.

   _____

3. no i will not be friends with liars.

   _____

4. yes i am being fair.

   _____

5. no i will not speak to her again.

   _____

WRITING AN INVITATION
Use the following form to invite someone to a party at your house.

_____

ADDRESSING AN ENVELOPE

Here is an envelope. Address it to the person you invited to your party.

_____

_____

_____

       _____

       _____

       _____

SPELLING

In the blanks, write each word with an **ing** ending and with an **ed** ending.

	ing ending	**ed** ending
1. rope	_____	_____
2. plan	_____	_____
3. fail	_____	_____
4. hop	_____	_____
5. stay	_____	_____
6. stop	_____	_____
7. pat	_____	_____
8. fan	_____	_____
9. show	_____	_____
10. chime	_____	_____

GO ON TO THE NEXT PAGE

SPELLING

These sentences have misspelled words. They do not make sense. Rewrite each sentence so that it makes sense. Spell each word correctly.

1. I did not no how to way myself at the fare.

   _____

2. I red that there is know right weigh to do that at the fare.

   _____

ALPHABETIZING

Write the following names in alphabetical order. Put commas between the names in the list you write.

Anne Lass   Charles Davis   Carol Lant   Joyce Mars   Richard Latt
Marie Mato   Judith Lamb   James Mase   George Law   Eve Larson
Betty Darbari   Henry Lave   Donald Laps   David Deare   Alice Lax

_____

_____

_____

_____

ALPHABETIZING (USING THE DICTIONARY)

Use the guide words **seal** and **send** to answer these questions. Write **Yes** or **No** in each blank.

1. Is the word **seem** on this page?   _____

2. Is the word **serve** on this page?   _____

3. Is the word **sell** on this page?   _____

4. Is the word **seven** on this page?   _____

5. Is the word **sale** on this page?   _____

STOP   CHECK YOUR ANSWERS BEGINNING ON PAGE 150.

Count how many items you answered correctly in each **Section** of the **Posttest**. Write your score per section in the **My Scores** column. If all of your section scores are as high as the **Good Scores**, go on to *Power English 4,* Chapter One. If any of your section scores are lower than the **Good Scores**, study the lessons on the assigned **Review Pages** again before you go on to *Power English 4,* Chapter One.

Section	Good Scores	My Scores	Review Pages
Capitalizing	4 or 5		2, 22, 44–45, 68, 98
Compound Subjects and Verbs in Sentences	4 or 5		23
Sentence Parts	4 or 5		5, 46
Recognizing Sentences	4 or 5		25
Combining Sentences	4 or 5		71, 99–100
Shortening Sentences with Commas	4 or 5		47, 48, 72, 73–74, 101, 102
Word Order in Sentences and Commas	4 or 5		49
Command Sentences	4 or 5		26
Recognizing Naming Words (Nouns)	8, 9, or 10		50
More Than One (Plural)	8, 9, or 10		6
The Pronouns **I**, **You**, **He**, **She**, **It**, **We**, and **They**	4 or 5		27, 28
The Pronouns **Him** and **Her** (Pronouns)	4 or 5		76
The Pronoun **Them**	4 or 5		108
Describing Words and Linking Words	4 or 5		103–104

Section	Good Scores	My Scores	Review Pages
Describing Words (Adjectives)	4 or 5		7
Action Words (Verbs)	4 or 5		8
The Verbs **Go**, **Goes**, **Went**, and **Will Go**	4 or 5		51, 52
The Verbs **Has**, **Have**, **Had** and **Will Have**	4 or 5		29
The Verbs **Do**, **Does**, **Did**, and **Will Do**	4 or 5		9
The Verbs **See**, **Sees**, **Saw**, and **Will See**	4 or 5		30, 31
Recognizing Describing Words (Adverbs)	4 or 5		10
Describing Words (Adverbs)	4 or 5		11, 53, 75, 105
Writing the Time of Day	4 or 5		57, 109, 110
Writing Dates	4 or 5		81
Writing Addresses	2		55–56
Shortening Words (Contractions)	8, 9, or 10		12, 13, 32, 77–78
The Words **A** and **An**	8, 9, or 10		33, 54
Using **Yes** and **No** in a Sentence	4 or 5		79–80
Writing an Invitation	A correct letter		82–83, 84–85
Addressing an Envelope	Correct addresses		113
Spelling	8, 9, or 10		58, 86, 114
Spelling	Both correct		14, 34
Alphabetizing	All correct		15, 35–36, 59, 87–88
Alphabetizing (Using the Dictionary)	4 or 5		115

ANSWERS

Chapter One
Capitalizing (Titles of Poems) (p. 2)

1. "To a Waterfowl" is a poem by William C. Bryant.
2. "When I Was One-and-Twenty" is a poem by A. E. Housman.
3. "The Road Not Taken" was written by Robert Frost.
4. "Meeting at Night" is a poem by Robert Browning.
5. "Go and Catch a Falling Star" is a poem by John Donne.

The Complete Subject of a Sentence (p. 3)

You should have a line under the following.
1. Chuck, Mike, and I
2. Mrs. Moran
3. The men, women, and children
4. Mr. St. Cloud and Mr. Burns
5. The train
6. A young child and her brother
7. A man and child
8. The storekeeper and a customer
9. The masked man
10. The gun and dog

Simple Subjects in Sentences (p. 4)

1. mother
2. Dogs, cats
3. Lions, apes, tigers
4. Robert, Diane, I
5. We

Recognizing Sentences (p. 5)

You should have a check by the following.
1. Don't play there.
2. You are the one in charge.
4. Stay.
5. He reads many books every year.
6. Takashi can't go.
7. The match is tomorrow.
10. Try that soon.

More Than One (Noun Plurals) (p. 6)

1. mice	8. flies	15. trays
2. children	9. men	16. bunnies
3. feet	10. women	17. cherries
4. geese	11. foxes	18. candies
5. teeth	12. churches	19. apples
6. bags	13. patches	20. passes
7. taxes	14. rashes	

Describing Words (Adjectives) (p. 7)

1. prettier	5. smarter	9. cleaner
2. nicest	6. honest	10. dirtier
3. happy	7. finest	
4. silliest	8. richest	

Action Words (Verbs) (p. 8)

1. played, will play	7. yelled, will yell
2. looked, will look	8. cried, will cry
3. tasted, will taste	9. carried, will carry
4. tried, will try	
5. cooked, will cook	10. prayed, will pray
6. joked, will joke	

The Verbs Do, Does, Did, and Will Do (p. 9)

1. do	5. did	9. will do
2. did	6. does	10. did
3. does	7. did	
4. will do	8. did	

Recognizing Describing Words (Adverbs) (p. 10)

You should have a line under the following.

1. carefully	5. fiercely	8. properly
2. softly	6. quickly	9. loudly
3. happily	7. cleverly	10. beautifully
4. noisily		

Recognizing Describing Words (Adverbs) (p. 11)

You should have a line under the following.

1. kindly	5. yesterday	8. today
2. early	6. promptly	9. tonight
3. late	7. soon	10. tomorrow
4. loudly		

Shortening Words (Contractions) (p. 12)

1. are not
2. could not
3. have not
4. is not
5. will not
6. didn't
7. shouldn't
8. hasn't
9. won't
10. don't

Shortening Words (Contractions) (p. 13)

1. it's
2. couldn't
3. she's
4. can't
5. won't
6. they're
7. we're
8. he's
9. hasn't
10. I'm

Spelling (p. 14)

1. tale
2. rode
3. wood
4. weigh
5. fare
6. tail
7. would
8. way
9. road
10. fair

Alphabetizing (p. 15)

1. cake, call, came, can, cape, cart, case, cat, cave
2. deal, debt, deck, deep, den, depth, desert, devil, dew
3. model, mole, mommy, month, more, most, moth, mouth, move
4. face, fade, faint, fake, fall, fame, fan, far, fat
5. safe, sag, sail, same, sane, sap, sat, save, saw

Chapter One Review
Capitalizing (Titles of Poems) (p. 16)

1. I enjoyed reading the poem "A Man and His Dog."
2. The poem "She Broke My Heart" is very sad.
3. My sister wrote the poem "Life Can Be Difficult."
4. I like funny poems like "My Upside Down Life."
5. "Blowing Bubbles at the World" is also very funny.

The Complete Subject of a Sentence (p. 16)

You should have a line under the following.
1. Tara, Carol, Matsue, and I
2. My pets
3. My boss, his wife, and their children
4. Two strange-looking men
5. My older sister and younger brother

Recognizing Sentences (pp. 16–17)

You should have a check by the following.
2. Go immediately.
3. They looked funny.

More Than One (Noun Plurals) (p. 17)

1. cookies
2. geese
3. women
4. teeth
5. babies
6. children
7. men
8. feet
9. mice
10. ladies

Describing Words (Adjectives) (p. 17)

1. noisier
2. silliest
3. dumbest
4. smarter
5. nicest

Action Words (Verbs) (p. 17)

1. jumped, will jump
2. looked, will look
3. landed, will land
4. baked, will bake
5. worked, will work

The Verbs Do, Does, Did, and Will Do (p. 18)

1. do
2. will do
3. did
4. do
5. did

Recognizing Describing Words (Adverbs) (p. 18)

You should have a line under the following.
1. today
2. carefully
3. suddenly
4. loudly
5. quickly
6. quietly
7. anxiously
8. noisily
9. immediately
10. slowly

Shortening Words (Contractions) (p. 18)

1. aren't
2. isn't
3. haven't
4. they're
5. she's
6. won't
7. can't
8. I'm
9. we're
10. you're

Spelling (p. 19)

1. I have the fare to go the fair.
2. Would you tell the child a tale?
3. They rode on the road to get to my house.
4. That would not be fair.
5. Which is the way to your house?

Alphabetizing (p. 19)

1. Colby, Combs, Cook, Fellini, Fermes, Forbes, Foster, Gates
2. Dean, Deitz, Delgado, Demo, Dermo, Drake, Drell, Dromer
3. Kant, Karro, Kashiwada, Katz, Kent, Kepler, Kramer, Krell
4. Saber, Sago, Samson, Sanchez, Sappo, Sardo, Sasso, Sato
5. Able, Ace, Acker, Adler, Alvarez, Amber, Anderson, Arrio

Chapter Two
Capitalizing (Titles of Poems and Stories) (p. 22)

1. Armin and I read "My Life Is a Bowl of Jelly" for the class.
2. Mr. and Mrs. Blake wrote the short story "Many Loves."
3. My favorite book is How to Fix Your House.
4. Franco's child likes the book The Cat in the Hat.
5. My sister has read "My Life Is Just a Dream" twice.

Compound Subjects in Sentences (p. 23)

1. e   Coffee and tea are common breakfast drinks.
2. h   Cereals and eggs are typical breakfast foods.
3. c   The lion and its trainer perform in a cage.
4. g   Dinosaurs and flying reptiles no longer exist.
5. a   Superman and Batman are comic book heroes.
6. b   Sun and water are needed for plants.
7. i   The bus and the train are ways to get to work.
8. j   Pepper and garlic make food taste better.
9. d   Lions and tigers are wild animals.
10. f   Oranges and lemons are citrus fruits.

Compound Verbs in Sentences (p. 24)

You should have lines under the following.
1. chased, grabbed
2. barked, snapped
3. stopped, watched
4. talked, stroked
5. dropped, swooped
6. opened, looked
7. slumped, moaned
8. tiptoed, touched
9. barked, frightened
10. dashed, played

Recognizing Sentences (p. 25)

You should have a check by the following.
1. Put that down.
2. Who said that?
5. Rose, Chuck, and Anita look happy.
6. They seem very quiet.
7. Show me how to do that.
8. Go.
9. Please stay a little longer.

Command Sentences (p. 26)

1. Stay.
   or: Stay!
2. Halt.
   or: Halt!
3. That is the best news I have ever heard!
4. Come down.
   or: Come down!
5. Put that down.
   or: Put that down!
6. Who took the tools?
7. Sue is leaving now.
8. Margaret is helping Frank learn to read.
9. I am leaving soon.
10. Please show that to me.

The Pronouns *I, You, He, She, It, We,* and *They* (p. 27)

1. I   2. She   3. They   4. We   5. They

The Pronouns *I, You, He, She, It, We,* and *They* (p. 28)

1. I	3. I	5. She	7. They	9. I
2. We	4. I	6. She	8. They	10. I

The Verbs *Had, Has, Have,* and *Will Have* (p. 29)

1. will have	5. has	8. will have
2. had	6. will have	9. had
3. have	7. has	10. have
4. has		

The Verbs *See, Sees, Saw,* and *Will See* (p. 30)

1. saw	5. will see	9. saw
2. saw	6. see	10. saw
3. sees	7. saw	
4. see	8. saw	

The Verbs *See, Sees, Saw,* and *Will See* (p. 31)

1. will see	5. saw	9. saw
2. see	6. saw	10. will see
3. saw	7. will see	
4. sees	8. will see	

Shortening Words (Contractions) (p. 32)

1. I'm	11. shouldn't
2. he's	12. they're
3. I'll	13. wouldn't
4. she'll	14. he'll
5. isn't	15. you'll
6. couldn't	16. hasn't
7. they'll	17. haven't
8. can't	18. aren't
9. won't	19. it's
10. we'll	20. didn't

The Words *A* and *An* (p. 33)

1. an unusual day	6. an ant
2. an umbrella	7. an upper floor
3. an open door	8. an underground safe
4. a pear	9. a bald man
5. an icy street	10. a unit price

Spelling (p. 34)

1. She would not go that way.
2. I read a good book an hour ago, too.
3. You are not going the right way to her house.
4. To be fair, the man gave each child bus fare.
5. No, I do not know the right person for the job.

Alphabetizing (pp. 35–36)

1. pack, pad, page, paid, party, past, peace, pen, pet, pretty, pride, pull, pure, push, put
2. sat, saw, seam, seem, sell, set, sit, soap, sold, some, sore, sue, suit, sum, sure
3. tar, tear, teeth, tick, tip, toe, too, top, tore, tour, trail, treat, trip, try, tub
4. wait, wall, was, water, wear, well, were, wet, whack, where, while, why, win, witch, won
5. ace, add, after, again, am, an, another, ant, ape, apple, are, arrest, ask, ate, aunt

Chapter Two Review
Capitalizing (Titles of Poems and Stories) (p. 37)

1. The story "The Canary Flew the Coop" is not about a bird.
2. "Making Duck Soup" is a silly story.
3. Herb and Sara wrote the story "Help Is on the Way."
4. How to Fix Everything is the best book I own.
5. I like the poem "I Need a Break."

Compound Subjects in Sentences (p. 37)

1. **b** An evil man and his wife stole a child from his parents.
2. **d** They wanted to sell the child to a childless couple.
3. **a** The child was only three months old.
4. **e** The parents and police waited for a phone call.
5. **c** The call never came.

Compound Verbs In Sentences (p. 38)

You should have a line under the following.
1. cried, begged
2. appeared, talked
3. saw, phoned
4. jumped, rushed
5. rescued, returned

Recognizing Sentences (p. 38)

You should have a check by the following.
1. Help is on the way.
2. Rush there immediately.

Command Sentences (p. 38)

1. Find that killer immediately.
   or: Find that killer immediately!
2. Please hold this for me.
3. Why did she do it?
4. You should not leave your baby alone outside.
5. Go.
   or: Go!

The Pronouns *I, You, He, She, It, We,* and *They* (pp. 38–39)

1. They 2. It 3. We 4. She 5. I

The Pronouns *I, You, He, She, It, We,* and *They* (p. 39)

1. I 2. They 3. They 4. I 5. We

The Verbs *Has, Have, Had,* and *Will Have* (p. 39)

1. has
2. had
3. will have
4. Have
5. had

The Verbs *See, Sees, Saw,* and *Will See* (p. 40)

1. saw
2. saw
3. will see
4. sees
5. saw
6. see
7. saw
8. see
9. will see
10. see

Shortening Words (Contractions) (p. 40)

1. I'll
2. they'll
3. we're
4. you'll
5. I'm
6. can't
7. she's
8. he'll
9. hasn't
10. we'll

The Words *A* and *An* (p. 40)

1. a union worker
2. a usual day
3. an honest person
4. a dark street
5. a green umbrella
6. a used car
7. a young man
8. a pink dress
9. an opera
10. an Easter bunny

Spelling (p. 41)

1. read
2. wood
3. Would
4. No; know
5. fare; fair

Alphabetizing (p. 41)

1. sack, search, sell, send, September, serious, set, seven, sew
2. cab, cafe, cage, cake, call, came, cane, cape, car
3. gas, gave, girl, give, gone, grass, green, grim, grow
4. tail, tale, that, these, this, train, tree, trip, try
5. baby, back, bad, bag, bail, bank, bar, base, bat

Chapter Three
Capitalizing (Names of Countries) (pp. 44–45)

1. Clara left Poland to come to the United States of America.
2. Harry S. White left Austria in June to come to America.
3. Mrs. I. Longo has lived in Iran, China, Japan, and France.
4. The Cramers and I traveled to Canada, Alaska, and Italy.
5. Ellen Tabrizi traveled to Russia, Ireland, Germany, and Spain.

Sentence Parts (p. 46)

1. **f** Jake is a new worker.
2. **d** My boss just hired Jake last week.
3. **a** The other workers are not very friendly to Jake.
4. **b** I am the only one talking to him.
5. **g** Which person will help him?
6. **c** My wife invited Jake's wife to our home.
7. **e** His wife had a good time at our house.
8. **j** It is not nice to be mean.
9. **h** No one should ignore anyone.
10. **i** Life is difficult enough.

Shortening Sentences with Commas (p. 47)

1. All my aunts, uncles, cousins, and grandparents visited me last week.
2. History, geography, and arithmetic are my favorite topics.
3. The workers, their families, and their bosses are at a picnic.
4. The birds, bees, and flowers tell me it is spring.
5. The monkeys, lions, tigers, and birds cannot be fed by zoo visitors.

Shortening Sentences with Commas (p. 48)

1. Turkey, chicken, and fish are what my doctor wants me to eat.
2. Ms. Rivera, Mr. Jordan, and Mrs. James are in business together.
3. The cake, ice cream, cookies, and candy you eat are high in sugar and fat.
4. The grapefruits, oranges, lemons, and limes were damaged in shipment.
5. Jerry, Tran, Adam, and Derrick work together.

Word Order in Sentences and Commas (p. 49)

1. Men, women, and children were at the picnic.
2. Mothers, fathers, children, and dogs ran into the woods.
3. Everyone heard a large growl.
4. The men, women, children, and dogs were frightened.
5. They saw a bear coming toward them.

Recognizing Naming Words (Nouns) (p. 50)

Last summer Pedro and his brother Sancho went to camp. The camp was in the country. Pedro was a lifeguard. His brother worked as his helper. There were many young children at the camp. During the year, the children all lived in the city. The children had never been out of the city. This was the first time they were in the country.

The camp had a small farm and garden. Some children had never seen a cow or a chicken. The children loved working in the garden. They also loved feeding the animals. Pedro, his brother, and all the children had a good time at camp.

The Verbs Go, Goes, Went, and Will Go (p. 51)

1. will go
2. goes
3. went
4. went
5. goes
6. went
7. will go
8. will go
9. will go
10. went

The Verbs Go, Goes, Went, and Will Go (p. 52)

1. will go
2. went
3. went
4. go
5. went
6. went
7. goes
8. went
9. will go
10. will go

Describing Words (Adverbs) (p. 53)

1. tomorrow
2. late
3. inside
4. outside
5. yesterday
6. away
7. nearby
8. now
9. here
10. suddenly

The Words A and An (p. 54)

1. a hand
2. a house
3. an hourglass
4. a union leader
5. a hungry worker
6. an hourly wage
7. a history lesson
8. an x-ray machine
9. a bottle
10. an ape
11. a sick person
12. a healthy animal
13. an unmade bed
14. a farmer
15. an idea
16. a mouse
17. an open door
18. a leaf
19. a chair
20. a hot tub

Writing Addresses (pp. 55–56)

1. José moved to Buffalo, New York.
2. Sandy has a new job in Reno, Nevada.
3. My parents live in Columbus, Ohio.
4. Are you going to Seattle, Washington?
5. Is your friend in Trenton, New Jersey?
6. My girlfriend lives in Little Rock, Arkansas.
7. Her grandparents recently moved to Miami, Florida.
8. Nader lives in Atlanta, Georgia.
9. Amy now lives in San Francisco, California.
10. Who recently left for Tulsa, Oklahoma?

Writing the Time of Day (p. 57)

1. 12:25 P.M.
2. 9:25 A.M.
3. 11:00 A.M.
4. 6:45 P.M.
5. 12:15 A.M.
6. 8:00 P.M.
7. 3.45 A.M.
8. 10:00 P.M.
9. 2:30 A.M.
10. 4:45 P.M.

Spelling (p. 58)

1. fitted
2. pinned
3. shopped
4. boiled
5. failed
6. dropped
7. petted
8. cooked
9. mailed
10. fanned
11. stopped
12. tanned
13. trapped
14. stepped
15. steamed
16. looked
17. chopped
18. broiled
19. chatted
20. filled

Alphabetizing (p. 59)

1. ant
2. bear
3. cake
4. call
5. can
6. cape
7. care
8. cave
9. cup
10. cure
11. cute
12. day
13. fat
14. girl
15. home
16. jail
17. man
18. name
19. near
20. net
21. night
22. one
23. only
24. pan
25. queen
26. quick
27. rich
28. run
29. seem
30. set
31. so
32. soap
33. son
34. sorry
35. sun
36. sure
37. up
38. wake
39. war
40. wax
41. were
42. what
43. when
44. while
45. why
46. won
47. x-ray
48. zoo

Chapter Three Review
Capitalizing (Names of Countries) (p. 60)

1. I dream of traveling to places such as Italy, Spain, and Greece.
2. Joe and I saved for two years to visit our parents in Poland.
3. I can only afford to travel to New Jersey from New York.
4. Andrew and I are going to France on our honeymoon.
5. Sara, Donna, Sonia, and I are going to China next summer.

Sentence Parts (p. 60)

1. c This Christmas will be a difficult one.
2. a I am out of work.
3. e My children need many things.
4. b My parents are very old.
5. d Only a miracle will make this a good Christmas.

Shortening Sentences with Commas (p. 61)

1. The dirty coat, sweater, and skirt need cleaning.
2. The Gerbers, Steins, and Benders are nice people.
3. The mother, father, brother, and sister look alike.
4. The dog, cat, and bird live with me.
5. The truck, car, and van couldn't get out of the mud.

Word Order in Sentences and Commas (p. 61)

1. Joanne, Marion, and I are good friends.
2. I need to buy vegetables, fruit, and fish.
3. Charles, Michael, and I visited China last year.
   or: Last year Charles, Michael, and I visited China.
4. Maria and I are going to Italy, Portugal, and Greece.
5. I would like to visit Hawaii, Bermuda, and Jamaica.

Naming Words (Nouns) (p. 62)

1. brothers
2. love
3. girl
4. family
5. result
6. boss
7. date
8. house
9. questions
10. parents

The Verbs *Go, Goes, Went,* and *Will Go* (p. 62)

1. went
2. will go
3. went
4. goes
5. go

Describing Words (Adverbs) (p. 63)

1. tomorrow
2. nearby
3. down
4. inside
5. suddenly

The Words *A* and *An* (p. 63)

1. an undergarment
2. a homemaker
3. a happy worker
4. an island
5. a history test
6. a tired person
7. an unusual person
8. a silly idea
9. an early date
10. an animal lover

Writing Addresses (pp. 63–64)

1. Artie and I are moving to Akron, Ohio.
2. The twins are building a house in Nashville, Tennessee.
3. My parents live in Brooklyn, New York.
4. My company is moving to Atlanta, Georgia.
5. I recently moved here from Detroit, Michigan.

Writing Time of Day (p. 64)

1. 4:10 A.M.
2. 10:00 P.M.
3. 3:05 A.M.
4. 12:45 P.M.
5. 7:15 A.M.

Spelling (p. 64)

1. fanned
2. petted
3. worked
4. spotted
5. jumped
6. dressed
7. banned
8. cried
9. topped
10. patted

Alphabetizing (p. 64)

an, answer, ant, bad, bag, bail, boil, bone, boss, both, bow, box, cab, call, came, cape, care, case, cat, cave, crawl, creep, crime, crow, face, fade, fail, fake, fall, fame, fan, far, fast, fat, favor, had, hall, ham, hand, happy

Chapter Four
Capitalizing (p. 68)

1. Mr. and Mrs. Alvin J. Warren were both born in May.
2. Karen A. Garcia and I are meeting on Monday.
3. The Boswells and the Murphys are coming here in March.
4. Ken L. Sato and Susan Hall are getting married on Tuesday.
5. Frank Valdo and Chris Kelly are going hunting in December.

Writing Sentences (pp. 69–70)

Sample Sentences:
1. My boss and his wife jog and swim every day.
2. The students and their dates dance and sing at parties.
3. The salesmen and their bosses talk and joke about many things.
4. The homeless man and woman eat and sleep at the shelter.
5. The fire fighters and police save lives and help many people.

Combining Sentences (p. 71)

1. Mallory studies, practices, and teaches piano.
2. Flores cooks, bakes, and irons well.
3. Barry works, exercises, and eats every day.
4. Emily teaches at school, plays the piano, and goes horseback riding.
5. The rain cleans the earth, waters the plants, and fills the lakes.

Shortening Sentences with Commas (p. 72)

1. The strikers carried signs, marched, and yelled.
2. They sang songs, drank coffee, and ate doughnuts.
3. The bosses ran the machines, answered the phones, and filled the orders.
4. The union leaders talked to the strikers, met with the bosses, and walked the picket line.
5. Passersby waved, talked, and smiled at the strikers.

Shortening Sentences with Commas (pp. 73–74)

1. Henri and Eleanor work, play, and go to school together.
2. Carlos read a book, listened to music, and talked to a friend last night.
3. We are taking canoeing, learning to swim, and joining a club next term.
4. The mechanics located, diagnosed, and fixed the problem.
5. We eat cereal, drink orange juice, and read the paper in the morning.

Describing Words (Adverbs) (p. 75)

1. happily
2. crazily
3. sadly
4. noisily
5. easily
6. steadily
7. strongly
8. highly
9. nicely
10. kindly

The Pronouns *Him* and *Her* (p. 76)

1. her
2. her
3. he
4. They
5. him
6. He
7. her
8. she
9. him
10. her

Shortening Words (Contractions) (pp. 77–78)

You should have a line under the following.

1. They've = They have
2. I'm = I am
3. She's = She has
4. we're = we are
5. they're = they are
6. I've = I have
7. It's = It is
8. She's = She is
9. He's = He has
10. She's = She is

Using *Yes* and *No* in a Sentence (pp. 79–80)

1. Yes, help is on the way.
2. Yes, I am happily married.
3. No, she does not want to go.
4. No, Mary did not say something else.
5. Yes, the room is very messy.
6. No, I do not like that dress.
7. Yes, everyone I know will be there.
8. Yes, I agree with you.
9. No, it is not too much.
10. Yes, it is too much for me.

Writing Dates (p. 81)

1. Beatrice moved to Texas on May 2, 1986.
2. Mike arrived in New York on July 17, 1987.
3. Hiro and Kimiko were married in Denver on April 13, 1978.
4. Michelle went to Philadelphia on January 20, 1988.
5. Kathy will move to Cleveland on September 14, 1989.

Writing an Invitation (pp. 82–83)

Sample Invitation:

> December 3, 1989
>
> Dear Joaquin,
>
> I'm having a birthday party for Jerry at my house on December 10, 1989, at 9:00 P.M. Please give me a call to let me know if you can come and to say how many people will come with you.
>
> Your friend,
> Floria

Writing an Invitation (pp. 84–85)

Sample Invitation:

> March 10, 1990
>
> Dear Ed,
>
> I'm having a get-together for a few friends at my home on March 25 at 8:00 P.M. I'll have lots of food, so don't eat dinner. I'd love to have you with us. Please phone to let me know if you can come. My number is 555-7219.
>
> Your friend,
> James

Spelling (p. 86)

1.	canning	11.	loading
2.	fitting	12.	sunning
3.	chatting	13.	letting
4.	sailing	14.	looking
5.	trimming	15.	stopping
6.	fanning	16.	grabbing
7.	wrapping	17.	trapping
8.	failing	18.	dialing
9.	trailing	19.	keeping
10.	chopping	20.	meeting

Alphabetizing (pp. 87–88)

1. Fred Gable, James Garcia, Jean Gerber, Martin Gomez, Hank Gonzalez, Betty Grable, Anthony Green, Seth Guzman
2. Joan Pace, Fred Pain, Ann Pane, Francis Parrot, Richard Patton, Don Payton, Sally Pear, John Powers
3. James Bear, Susan Dale, Marcie Daniels, Gloria Davis, Edward Dean, Donna Dempsy, Charles Donne, Fred Drake
4. Lawrence Saab, Carol Sable, Kenneth Sachs, Frank Sallo, George Samley, José Sanchez, Frank Sartino, Maria Satos
5. Cynthia Baker, Alice Bennett, Angela Booker, Daniel Braun, Robert Breck, Donald Brine, Kathleen Brown, Walter Brunn

Chapter Four Review
Capitalizing (p. 89)

1. My fiancé and I can't afford a big wedding.
2. We are getting married in June and moving to California.
3. Our parents live in Maine and are upset about our moving to California.
4. My parents' friends, Mr. and Mrs. S. Shibata, helped us a lot.
5. March, April, and May will be very busy months for Betty and me.

Writing Sentences (pp. 89–90)

Sample Sentences:
1. George and I returned home and relaxed.
2. The old man and his wife enjoy life and do lots of things.
3. My girlfriend and her sister dance and sing very well.
4. The hungry child and her brother cried and asked for food.
5. Greg and his family argue and fight a lot.

Combining Sentences (p. 90)

1. The twins work, play, and stay together.
2. That man looks, acts, and seems very strange.
3. The homeless man screamed, jumped, and cursed at people.
4. The lost child ate some food, drank some soda, and played with the police officer.
5. The child's mother searched for her child, cried, and went to the police.

Shortening Sentences with Commas (p. 91)

1. The city can be an exciting, great, and fun place to live.
2. The city can also be an unfriendly, dangerous, and frightening place to live.
3. Dan drinks, smokes, and works too much.
4. My job tires, bores, and depresses me a lot.
5. I want to get married, raise a family, and have a nice house.

Describing Words (Adverbs) (p. 91)

1.	sadly	6.	swiftly
2.	slowly	7.	quickly
3.	carefully	8.	shortly
4.	proudly	9.	happily
5.	gladly	10.	angrily

The Pronouns *Him* and *Her* (p. 91)

1.	him	3.	her	5.	him
2.	her	4.	him		

Shortening Words (Contractions) (p. 92)

1. cannot
2. has not
3. have not
4. they have
5. it is **or** it has
6. I will
7. she is **or** she has
8. I have
9. she will
10. they are

Using *Yes* and *No* in a Sentence (p. 92)

1. No, I can't stay.
2. Yes, Benita will be here soon.
3. Yes, that is very nice.
4. No, she is not being fair.
5. Yes, I will marry Bill.

Writing Dates (p. 92)

1. May 4, 1990
2. February 11, 1932
3. November 3, 1927
4. August 9, 1941
5. January 1, 1988

Writing an Invitation (p. 93)

Sample Invitation:

> February 7, 1990
> Dear Hank and Beth,
>   Phillip and I are having a birthday party for Alan on Saturday, February 20, at our home. The fun should begin about 7:30 P.M. We'd like everyone to bring a special dish.
>   Please phone to let us know if you can come. We can also talk about what you would like to bring. Our phone number is (609) 882-3168.
>
> Your friends,
> Phillip and Tara

Spelling (p. 93)

1. running
2. petting
3. hitting
4. wrapping
5. spotting
6. playing
7. getting
8. setting
9. trapping
10. planning

Alphabetizing (p. 94)

Sally Abrams, Dale Ackers, Alice Addison, Jack Adler, Susan Cramer, Richard Drake, Donald Dreyer, Sally Dugan, Frank May, Frank Means, George Mebber, Dorothy Mecker, Alan Meeker, David Meger, Alvin Mein, Mary Meklo, Joseph Melm, Sam Memer, Sara Ment, José Mondez

Chapter Five
Capitalizing (p. 98)

1. My sister and I share an apartment on River Avenue in Boston.
2. She and I moved here from Detroit last August.
3. Our divorced parents moved from France to the United States.
4. Our mother, Mrs. Audrey Adams, remarried and lives in New Jersey.
5. Our father, Mr. Anthony Brandt, lives in Washington, D.C.

Combining Sentences (pp. 99–100)

1. Sally, Mark, and Pedro love to dance.
2. Mr. McCall, Miss Otis, and Ms. Franco live on Main Street.
3. My mother, father, and sister are nice.
4. This pig, cow, and goat live on a farm.
5. Mrs. Meltzer, Valerie, and Ali are happy.

Shortening Sentences with Commas (p. 101)

You should have rewritten the following.

2. At night the city looks dark, lonely, and frightening.
3. My boyfriend is a charming, handsome, and clever man.
5. I seem dull, crabby, and ugly next to him.

Shortening Sentences with Commas (p. 102)

1. The snow was white, clean, and deep.
2. The robber was masked, tall, and fat.
3. The robber's dog was filthy, stinking, and dangerous.
4. The police were brave, strong, and caring.
5. The victims were frightened, upset, and tired.

Describing Words and Linking Words (pp. 103–104)

You should have a line under the following.

1. young; worried; afraid
2. unlined; pale; tight
3. pretty; calm; joyful
4. proud; tense; confused
5. jolly; pleased; happy
6. impatient; uneasy
7. tired; unhappy
8. lovely; beautiful
9. large; empty
10. happy

Describing Words (Adverbs) (p. 105)

1. proudly
2. carefully
3. quietly
4. clearly
5. beautifully
6. cheerfully
7. swiftly
8. rudely
9. carelessly
10. loudly

Describing Words (Adjectives and Adverbs) (pp. 106–107)

1. The beautiful lady ate slowly.
2. The small plane landed safely.
3. My good friend arrived yesterday.
4. My smart girlfriend speaks softly.
5. His tired boss will work tomorrow.
6. The old dog barked weakly.
7. The frightened person screamed loudly.
8. My handsome boyfriend dances nicely.
9. The small animal drinks quickly.
10. A good pilot flies carefully.

The Pronoun *Them* (p. 108)

1. them
2. They
3. them
4. them
5. they
6. them
7. them
8. them
9. They
10. them

Writing the Time of Day (p. 109)

1. 8:30 A.M.
2. 4:20 P.M.
3. 6:00 P.M.
4. 11:30 A.M.
5. 6:15 A.M.
6. 11:00 P.M.
7. 4:00 A.M.
8. 3:10 A.M.
9. 5:05 P.M.
10. 1:45 P.M.

Writing the Time of Day (p. 110)

1. I am getting up at 8:30 A.M. tomorrow.
2. Do you want me to awaken you at 6:45 A.M.?
3. Will you be able to leave work at 5:50 P.M.?
4. Is it 11:00 P.M. already?
5. Patty and Kim are arriving at 10:45 A.M.

Writing a Friendly Letter (pp. 111–112)

Sample Letter:

> May 23, 1990
> Dear Ron,
>   Thank you for inviting me to your party. I had a fabulous time! The food was delicious, and the people were lots of fun.
>   Your friend,
>   Colette

Addressing and Envelope (p. 113)

Sample Envelope:

```
Colette Brooks
64 Baker Street
Pittsburgh, Pennsylvania 15230

        Ron Andrews
        369 Louis Drive
        Pittsburgh, Pennsylvania 15224
```

Spelling (p. 114)

1. blaming
2. coming
3. hoping
4. making
5. hopping
6. running
7. faking
8. raking
9. sitting
10. waking
11. boiling
12. fanning
13. sitting
14. burning
15. stopping
16. filing
17. keeping
18. taking
19. stating
20. filling

Alphabetizing (Using the Dictionary) (p. 115)

1. Yes
2. No
3. No
4. Yes
5. No
6. Yes
7. No
8. No
9. Yes
10. Yes

Chapter Five Review
Capitalizing (p. 116)

1. Miss Anne J. Kelly lives on West Street in Detroit.
2. On Tuesday Mr. and Mrs. Alvin J. Cole are going to Miami, Florida.
3. On Friday Ms. Moon and I are driving to Atlanta, Georgia.
4. Mr. Ortez and Miss Torres came to New York City from Spain.
5. Eduardo, Julio, Ruby, and I are leaving on Wednesday for Italy.

Combining Sentences (pp. 116–117)

1. Gregory, Mariquita, and Seth do well in everything.
2. Yoshiko, Laura, and Terry live in California.
3. David, Brad, and Gloria just bought clothes.
4. Henry, Margaret, and I won the lottery.
5. The animals, men, and women look frightened.

Shortening Sentences with Commas (p. 117)

1. The play was funny, sad, and different.
2. That man is handsome, tall, and smart.
3. Kerry seems lonely, frightened, and worried.
4. The clown looks old, sad, and tired.
5. Mack is angry, annoyed, and unhappy.

Describing Words and Linking Words (p. 117)

You should have a line under the following.

1. unhappy; tired
2. old; sad
3. angry
4. rude; mean
5. handsome; young

Describing Words (Adverbs) (p. 118)

1. correctly
2. cruelly
3. calmly
4. crudely
5. carefully
6. fiercely
7. meanly
8. joyfully
9. carelessly
10. clearly

The Pronoun *Them* (p. 118)

1. them
2. They
3. them
4. they; them
5. They

Writing the Time of Day (p. 118)

1. 9:15 P.M.
2. 2:10 A.M.
3. 1:30 P.M.
4. 11:25 P.M.
5. 4:05 A.M.

Writing a Friendly Letter (p. 119)

Sample Letter:

> September 5, 1990
> Dear Bob,
>   It was very kind of you to take me to lunch yesterday. I enjoyed it very much. You really know how to pick great places to eat.
>   Thanks again.
>
>   Fondly,
>   Jill

Addressing an Envelope (p. 119)

Sample Envelope:

```
Jill Morgan
325 River Road
Arlington, Virginia 22210

          Robert Allington
          47 Farm Drive
          Arlington, Virginia 22203
```

Spelling (p. 120)

1. raking
2. taking
3. making
4. greeting
5. hitting
6. timing
7. walking
8. hating
9. crying
10. piling

Alphabetizing (Using the Dictionary) (p. 120)

1. Yes
2. No
3. Yes
4. No
5. No

Posttest
Capitalizing (p. 123)

1. Mr. and Mrs. Oliver M. Collins live on York Avenue in Dallas, Texas.
2. Ms. Anderson and her friend Carla are visiting Italy and Spain next winter.
3. Have you read "My Life Is an Open Book"?
4. The poem "I'm an Only Child and I Love It" is very funny.
5. The Silbys moved in September from Washington, D.C., to Omaha, Nebraska.

Compound Subjects and Verbs in Sentences (p. 123)

You should have one line under the following.
1. twins; wives
2. friends; wives
3. Herbert; Jack
4. nieces; nephews
5. they

You should have two lines under the following.
1. work; travel
2. mistake
3. talk; walk
4. love; adore
5. live; work

Sentence Parts (p. 124)

1. **d** Hate can only destroy.
2. **c** Love can heal many wounds.
3. **a** I like cheerful people.
4. **e** A gloomy person is no fun to be with.
5. **b** Holidays are lonely for people without friends.

Recognizing Sentences (p. 124)

You should have a check by the following.
3. Rush there.
4. Try to come early.
5. Please stay a little longer.

Combining Sentences (pp. 124–125)

1. The fruit looks, smells, and tastes good now.
2. Betty wears very pretty dresses, hats, and sweaters.
3. My car needs new seat covers, tires, and windows.
4. The police chased, arrested, and handcuffed the robber.
5. The Chins walk, talk, and eat fast.

Shortening Sentences with Commas (p. 125)

1. Mr. Charm, Mr. Chase, and I get up early every morning.
2. My brother Peter, my sister Heather, and I exercise every day.
3. Marie, Judy, and Rebecca often swim at the YWCA.
4. My kitchen, bedroom, and bathroom need painting badly.
5. James, William, and Robert want to work overtime tomorrow.

Word Order in Sentences and Commas (p. 126)

1. Scott, Jeff, and I are working overtime today.
2. Andy, Dave, and Hossein are going away this weekend.
3. Juanita, Ann, and I are giving a New Year's party.
4. We are going to visit my aunts, uncles, and parents.
5. At school I am learning reading, writing, and arithmetic.
   or: I am learning reading, writing, and arithmetic at school.

Command Sentences (p. 126)

1. Hold that door.
   or: Hold that door!
2. Stand back.
   or: Stand back!
3. Please give her some room.
4. What are you doing?
5. She is fabulous!

Recognizing Naming Words (Nouns) (p. 126)

You should have a line under the following.

I met my <u>wife</u> at <u>school</u>. She dropped her <u>books</u>, <u>papers</u>, <u>pens</u>, and <u>pencils</u> on the <u>floor</u> next to me. I stopped to help her. When I looked up, I saw this beautiful, smiling <u>face</u>. I fell in <u>love</u> with her immediately. All <u>day</u> I could only think about her.

More Than One (Plural) (p. 127)

1. women
2. teeth
3. men
4. houses
5. geese
6. tables
7. mice
8. children
9. ladies
10. classes

The Pronouns *I*, *You*, *He*, *She*, *It*, *We*, and *They* (p. 127)

1. It
2. We
3. I
4. He
5. They

The Pronouns *Him* and *Her* (p. 127)

1. him
2. her
3. her
4. She
5. him

The Pronoun *Them* (p. 128)

1. them
2. them
3. they
4. They
5. them

Describing Words and Linking Words (p. 128)

You should have a line under the following.
1. lovely young; charming
2. pretty; kind
3. beautiful; fresh
4. tiny; pointed
5. three; mean; ugly

Describing Words (Adjectives) (p. 128)

1. bigger
2. fattest
3. prettier
4. nicest
5. finest

Action Words (Verbs) (pp. 128–129)

1. played; will play
2. cleaned; will clean
3. looked; will look
4. rushed; will rush
5. turned; will turn

The Verbs *Go*, *Goes*, *Went*, and *Will Go* (p. 129)

1. went
2. will go
3. went
4. will go
5. goes

The Verbs *Has*, *Have*, *Had*, and *Will Have* (p. 129)

1. has
2. had
3. had
4. has
5. will have

The Verbs *Do*, *Does*, *Did*, and *Will Do* (p. 129)

1. will do
2. did
3. do
4. did
5. does

The Verbs *See*, *Sees*, *Saw*, and *Will See* (p. 130)

1. will see
2. saw
3. see
4. will see
5. see

Recognizing Describing Words (Adverbs) (p. 130)

You should have a line under the following.
1. yesterday
2. freely
3. everywhere
4. yesterday; today
5. peacefully

Describing Words (Adverbs) (p. 130)

1. carelessly
2. fiercely
3. shortly
4. brightly
5. cleverly
6. finely
7. hopefully
8. nicely
9. stupidly
10. meanly

Writing the Time of Day (pp. 130–131)

1. 1:15 A.M.
2. 3:20 P.M.
3. 9:45 P.M.
4. 7:30 P.M.
5. 11:10 A.M.

Writing Dates (p. 131)

1. June 25, 1988
2. October 3, 1983
3. April 8, 1917
4. November 10, 1989
5. July 4, 1942

Writing Addresses (p. 131)

1. 874 Perry Street
   Atlanta, Georgia 30351
2. 34 Second Avenue
   Santa Fe, New Mexico 87505

Shortening Words (Contractions) (p. 131)

1. I'll
2. hasn't
3. she'll
4. they're
5. couldn't
6. don't
7. he's
8. I've
9. we'll
10. doesn't

The Words *A* and *An* (p. 131)

1. a huge house
2. a union card
3. an hourly job
4. a young person
5. an ulcer
6. a high fence
7. a hot plate
8. an underwater watch
9. an ear
10. an unused ticket

Using *Yes* and *No* in a Sentence (p. 132)

1. No, Sally and I are not friends.
2. Yes, she lies a lot.
3. No, I will not be friends with liars.
4. Yes, I am being fair.
5. No, I will not speak to her again.

Writing an Invitation (p. 132)

Sample Invitation:

> April 24, 1990
> Dear Libby,
>   I'm having a housewarming party Sunday, May 10, starting at 3:00 P.M. I hope you'll be able to come. I'm looking forward to seeing you. My new address is 32 Maple Avenue.
>   Please phone me at 555-3607 by May 6.
> Your friend,
> Patrick

Addressing an Envelope (p. 133)

Sample Envelope:

```
Patrick Mahoney
32 Maple Avenue
Oakland, California 94618

        Libby Smith
        3689 Beaver Road
        Oakland, California 94624
```

Spelling (p. 133)

1. roping; roped
2. planning; planned
3. failing; failed
4. hopping; hopped
5. staying; stayed
6. stopping; stopped
7. patting; patted
8. fanning; fanned
9. showing; showed
10. chiming; chimed

Spelling (p. 134)

1. I did not know how to weigh myself at the fair.
2. I read that there is no right way to do that at the fair.

Alphabetizing (p. 134)

Betty Darbari, Charles Davis, David Deare, Judith Lamb, Carol Lant, Donald Laps, Eve Larson, Anne Lass, Richard Latt, Henry Lave, George Law, Alice Lax, Joyce Mars, James Mase, Marie Mato

Alphabetizing (Using the Dictionary) (p. 134)

1. Yes   2. No   3. Yes   4. No   5. No